SEVEN
REVOLUTIONS

For Further Reading

OTHER BOOKS BY MIKE AQUILINA

Roots of the Faith: From the Church Fathers to You

Yours Is the Church: How Catholicism Shapes Our World

The Fathers of the Church

The Mass of the Early Christians

Signs and Mysteries: Revealing Ancient Christian Symbols

The Mass: The Glory, the Mystery, the Tradition
(with Cardinal Donald Wuerl)

OTHER BOOKS BY JIM PAPANDREA

ROME: A Pilgrim's Guide to the Eternal City

Trinity 101: Father, Son, Holy Spirit

*Reading the Early Church Fathers:
From the Didache to Nicaea*

*Novatian of Rome and the Culmination
of Pre-Nicene Orthodoxy*

*The Wedding of the Lamb: A Historical
Approach to the Book of Revelation*

*Spiritual Blueprint: How We Live, Work,
Love, Play, and Pray*

SEVEN
REVOLUTIONS

*How Christianity Changed the World
and Can Change It Again*

MIKE AQUILINA

AND

JAMES L. PAPANDREA

IMAGE

New York

Copyright © 2015 by Michael Aquilina and James L. Papandrea

All rights reserved.
Published in the United States by Image,
an imprint of the Crown Publishing Group,
a division of Random House LLC,
a Penguin Random House Company, New York.
www.crownpublishing.com

IMAGE is a registered trademark and the "I" colophon is
a trademark of Random House LLC.

Library of Congress Cataloging-in-Publication Data is available
upon request.

ISBN 978-0-8041-3896-3
eBook ISBN 978-0-8041-3897-0

Printed in the United States of America

Cover design by Jessie Sayward Bright
Cover illustration by Bridgeman Art Library

10 9 8 7 6 5 4 3 2 1

First Edition

To our friends and colleagues

who pave the way and open doors for us,

who support us, encourage us, challenge us, stretch us,

who read our work and give us good counsel.

You know who you are.

Contents

A Note on the Text

Many of our quotations from the Fathers are adapted from the three great nineteenth-century translation series, The Fathers of the Church, The Ante-Nicene Fathers, and the Nicene and Post-Nicene Fathers. We have updated the language to make it readable for our contemporaries.

CHAPTER 1

THE CHURCH OF THE FUTURE CAN LEARN FROM THE CHURCH OF THE PAST

The bishop was led into the stadium, where death and gore were entertainment, and where the crowd was hoping to drown the harsh realities of life, and the fear of their own mortality, in someone else's blood. Three days earlier, Bishop Polycarp had dreamed that his pillow was on fire. He knew that meant soon he was going to face the flames. Now, as he entered the arena in chains, surrounded by those who hated the faith that he stood for, he heard the voice of God encouraging him, telling him to be strong and courageous. When the crowd saw him and recognized him as the leader of the Christians in their city, they cheered to see that he had been arrested.

Polycarp stood before the Roman proconsul, the man whom the emperor had sent to be the governor of the province. When asked, Polycarp confirmed that he was indeed the bishop of the city of Smyrna. This was as good as an admission of guilt. Being a Christian was not only illegal; it was considered an antisocial, even treasonous, crime—and, therefore, it was a crime worthy of death.

The proconsul attempted to convince Polycarp to deny his faith to save his life. "You're an old man," he pleaded, implying that the ordeal Polycarp faced would be all the more harsh because of his age. "All you have to do is take an oath to the emperor . . . and renounce your fellow traitors." Because Christians worshipped only one God, instead of the many gods of the Greco-Roman pantheon, the non-Christians took to calling Christians "atheists." The proconsul promised Polycarp that he would go free if he would only deny his faith and his Christian community by saying, "Away with the atheists." In response, the bishop of Smyrna turned to the pagan crowd, pointed to them, and said, "Away with the atheists!"

Angered, but wishing to make an apostate rather than a martyr, the Roman proconsul pressed again, "Swear the oath, and I will release you. . . . Curse Christ!" But Polycarp calmly replied, "I have been his servant for eighty-six years, and he has done me no wrong. How can I blaspheme my King, who saved me?" As the proconsul continued to rail at the bishop, Polycarp went on, "If you think that I will do as you request and swear an oath to Caesar, pretending not to know who I am, then listen carefully: I am a Christian. Now if you want to learn the teachings of Christianity, set a day and give me a hearing."

Eventually, the proconsul took a different tack. He threatened that wild animals would tear Polycarp apart while the spectators cheered. But the bishop responded, "Call for them. To change one's mind from

evil to righteousness is a good thing, but to go from bet-
ter to worse is something we cannot do." The proconsul
responded, "If you're not afraid of the wild beasts, I
will have you burned with fire, unless you change your
mind." Polycarp replied, "You threaten me with a fire
that burns for only a little while and then is put out. But
you know nothing of the eternal fire, the eternal punish-
ment that awaits the ungodly at the coming judgment.
Why do you hesitate? Come on, do what you will!"

Members of the crowd eagerly helped gather wood
for the fire, and as the bishop prayed, the fire was
lit. Although the flames surrounded him, the saintly
bishop's body was not consumed. Finally a soldier was
ordered to kill him with a dagger. The wound produced
so much blood that the crowd looked on in amazement
as Polycarp's blood put out the fire. But the bishop was
dead. The fire was lit once again, and Polycarp's body
was burned to prevent its veneration. But the faithful
of Smyrna were able to retrieve his bones, which were
treated as holy relics [1]

What kind of culture encourages people to cheer at the death of an elderly man who is guilty of no other crime than being a Christian bishop? And how did human-ity progress from the Roman culture of Polycarp's time to the kind of people we are now, feeling surprise, horror, and disgust with such martyr stories? What changed in human society to make us what we are today? And is there evidence that we as a culture could be slipping back to where we once were? This book is about seven cultural revolutions that changed human society for the better. These revolutions are the direct result of the presence of Christianity in the world, and of the influence of the Christian Church on society. But in a time when it has become fashionable once again to cheer the misfortunes of the Church, and to highlight the Church's failures as if they over-shadow its faithfulness, it is important to point out the ways in which Christianity has made the world a better place, and to demonstrate that these far outweigh the times when a few leaders of the Church have failed in their mission. The truth is, the best of human society, with its improved quality of life, and its protection of human rights, is the result of these seven cultural revolutions that came about because of the Christian Church. Specifically, these revolutions were a radical change in the way human society thought of the individual, the fam-ily, work, religion, community, attitudes toward life and death, and even government.

These seven revolutions have brought about a real trans-formation in the way people see themselves and their relation-ships with one another—a conversion that first took place by the implementation of the values of the Gospel in the early Christian Church and later extended to the surrounding cul-ture. Another way to look at it is that the seven revolutions were corrections of certain flaws in ancient society in general, and Roman society in particular. For example, in the ancient world, a person's worth was based on what he or she might produce, or how he or she might be a burden to others. It was Christianity that would give the world a sense of the intrinsic value of every human being. In other words, in the worldview of ancient cultures, some people were expendable, and some people were property. Furthermore, in the Roman Empire the enjoyment of quality of life (along with the freedoms and free time that make that possible) was a luxury afforded to the rich. Both religion and government existed to serve the ruling classes, which created a hopelessness in the lower classes and a tendency toward selfish hedonism in the upper classes. These flaws of ancient culture are generalizations, to a certain extent, but they do describe the world into which Christianity was born.

The seven revolutions, then, were both a response to the Gospel, and a rejection of the cultural values that were in conflict with the teachings of Jesus and the apostles. The early Church was nothing if not countercultural, to the extent that even slaves and former slaves could become bishops. As we present them here, the seven revolutions changed the world by changing human relationships, in ever widening concentric circles, beginning with the individual and extending outward to the world. A revolution of the individual affirmed that all people are created equal, in the image of God, and no one is expendable. A revolution of the home affirmed it as a place of safety and love, where women and children are not to be exploited. A revolution of the workplace affirmed that people are not property, that they must be free to choose their work, and that they must be given the free time for worship, for artistic expression, and to enjoy their loved ones. A revolution of religion taught the world that God is love. A revolution of the community taught people to love their neighbor. A revolution of the way people thought about life and death rejected the culture of death and affirmed a culture of life and of hope, encouraging people to stand up for human rights. And finally, a revolution of government set up the ideal that rulers should serve those whom they rule (not the other way around), and that all people should enjoy freedom of religion. In short, the seven revolutions can be understood as cultural revolutions that gave the world a concern for human rights in two general categories: the protection of all human life, and the protection of each person's dignity and freedom.

To be sure, these revolutions are built on the foundation of Judaism, the religion of Jesus and the apostles. But it was the Christian Church that expanded on the teachings of Judaism (such as the concept that all humans are created in the image of God), took the implications of those teachings into the world, and converted the world to a new way of looking at humanity and human relationships. The seven revolutions did not occur overnight. The conversion of the world was a long process, beginning during the Roman Empire. Some of the revolutions were already under way in the first few centuries of the Church, in spite of the fact that Christianity was still illegal and Christians were being persecuted. Some of the changes had to wait until the legalization of Christianity, at which point the Church could begin to convert the empire from the inside. Other revolutions took longer and required controversies within the Church to bring the Church to certain conclusions about how the teachings of Jesus were to be lived. The result is that by the Middle Ages, Christianity had shaped Western culture, and it would continue to influence culture wherever the Gospel spread. And although it is easy to name instances in which Christians have not lived up to the ideals of the Church, it is only because the Church gave us those ideals that we can now recognize and critique such human failures. In other words, without the precedents that Christianity established with regard to the protection of life, dignity, and freedom, we would have no standards by which to judge any person or group (including the Church itself) that fails to protect human rights.

Therefore, seeing things in terms of the big picture, it is important to understand just how much the Church has improved the quality of human life. This book will offer some examples of the many positive contributions the Church has made to the conversion of human culture. Finally, we will show why understanding the seven revolutions is so important for the Church (and the world) today, and we'll offer some concrete steps that can be taken by Christians in the twenty-first century. But before we can get to that, we need to understand the Church of Polycarp's time.

The Pre-Christian World

When we refer to the "pre-Christian" world, we don't mean the world before Christianity came along. We mean the world before Christianity converted it—the world in which Christianity was a persecuted, illegal religion. The Christian Church was born in the Roman Empire. At that time, the "known world" was an empire that stretched from Spain to Israel and surrounded the Mediterranean Sea. Christianity emerged on the far eastern end of that empire and spread all the way across to the western end remarkably quickly, in the midst of a wide range of diverse religions that were being practiced in the vast region. Yet, as a religion, Christianity was different from anything that had come before it. In part, this is because the world had yet to see a religion that combined an open membership policy with strict moral expectations. Anyone was invited to join the Church, but once a person joined they were expected to make a serious commitment to changing their lifestyle. Judaism had moral expectations, but like most of the ancient world's religions, Judaism was essentially the religion of a particular nation; you belonged because you were born into it. Many of the so-called mystery cults (secret societies with initiation rituals, often imported from the provinces of the empire) eventually became ethnically inclusive, so they were not limited to one tribe or nation, but they tended to be relatively homogeneous in terms of the social class or sex of their members. Some groups were open only to women, or only to men, such as the cult of Mithras. We have no evidence that these cults placed any expectations on a member's behavior outside of the rituals in which members participated.

For the most part, traditional Roman religion centered on civic duty—those who participated were not held to a code of morality or required to hold certain beliefs. The priests of the Roman cults were not concerned with what you did behind closed doors, as long as you kept to a minimum level of public decorum, and an acceptable level of patriotic loyalty. The practical exercise of patriotism in the Roman Empire was the imperial cult, in which citizens were expected to make sacrifices to the gods in honor of, or in the name of, the emperor. At the same time, the emperors were following Egyptian precedent and increasingly claiming divine titles for themselves. Julius Caesar claimed to be descended from the gods, and when he died, the Roman Senate proclaimed him divine. Once he was declared to be a god, his nephew and heir, Augustus, claimed to be the son of a god. This trend continued until it came to a high point at the end of the first century with the emperor Domitian, who demanded to be called, "lord and god."[2] Christians and non-Christians alike understood that they were expected to engage in emperor worship, as cultic images of the emperors, and even temples dedicated to the emperors, went up all over the empire.

Christians naturally believed that participating in any pagan worship was idolatry. But the Roman government saw their refusal to be part of the imperial cult as an act of treason, and treason was punishable by death. So the friction between the Christian Church and the Roman government centered on a conflict of loyalties—Christ or Caesar. Conversion to Christianity could not be tolerated because it replaced loyalty to Caesar with obedience to Christ, replacing the empire of the Romans with the kingdom of heaven.

Thus, contrary to popular misconception, the Romans were not tolerant when it came to religion. While they did generally allow conquered people to retain their national or tribal religions (to prevent revolt), the Romans were accepting of foreign cults only to a point. New religions were always suspect, and the extent to which Christianity was seen as something new (as opposed to being a sect of Judaism) worked against the Church in the eyes of the Romans. Other religions were treated with suspicion as well. Certain Egyptian cults were suppressed, and the Senate even tried to legislate against the wild celebrations of some of the mystery cults, such as the cults of Cybele and Bacchus.[3] The Druids were outlawed, understandably, for practicing human sacrifice. And in the third century, an emperor outlawed the Roman version of the Masonic lodge, a gnostic secret society known as Manichaeism. So, in reality, a person was free to add gods to their personal pantheon only as long as the accompanying practices did not include unruly public behavior or suspicious secret activities. And no one was free to ignore the traditional gods that protected the empire, nor were they free to opt out of the imperial cult. The Christians could not fulfill these cultural expectations, so they were among those who did not enjoy religious freedom.[4]

In Roman culture, the concept of freedom amounted to an entitlement to self-indulgence for the wealthy and powerful (those with leisure time). The belief that one deserved one's station in life allowed the wealthy to justify an entirely hedonistic lifestyle, including the abuse of others whose station in life did not afford them protection from exploitation. It was in this context that the Romans first noticed that the Christian Church required that its members reject Greco-Roman religions, as well as the exploitive personal freedoms that powerful Romans cherished. Rather than following the lead of the culture, the Christians followed the example of Jesus, who had compassion for the powerless, and who had said that following him would mean self-denial, not self-indulgence (Matthew

16:24–26). Christian writers openly criticized Roman society for its superstition and hedonism. This, combined with Christians' refusal to participate in traditional Roman religion, meant that to pagan Romans, Christians seemed rigorously intolerant, and the Church came to be seen as downright antisocial.

Jesus warned that his followers should expect to be persecuted (Matthew 5:11–12; 10:16–39; 24:9–13), and indeed they were. Beginning with the precedent set by Nero in Rome in the midsixties of the first century, Roman law increasingly targeted Christians, and especially the leaders of the Church.[5] By the end of the first century, Christians were tortured and executed simply for admitting to being followers of Christ. The Church came to see itself as inherently opposed to (and opposed by) the culture around it—as we would say, it was countercultural. This distinction became part of the identity of the Church in the first few centuries of its existence. Ignatius of Antioch, writing in the early second century, said that "Christianity is greatest when it is hated by the world."[6]

In the middle of the third century, the Roman Empire was about two hundred eighty years old (having changed from a republic to an empire as it emerged from civil war in the decades before the birth of Christ). In fact, it was not too much older than the United States is now. The economy of the empire was in a serious recession as the result of uncontrollable inflation and multiple wars in the region we now call the Middle East. Currency was devalued, yet the emperors increasingly had to spend money they didn't have on bureaucracy, and on the military and its infrastructure. Unemployment and underemployment were increasing exponentially as large

landholders took over the small farms and forced the landless
into the cities. The average family size decreased as children
came to be seen as more of a liability than an asset. Nomadic
people (the "barbarians") were crossing the borders and coming into the empire. And as a way to escape from the brutality
of everyday life, the brutality of real violence and death was
offered up as a spectator sport. All of this sounds familiar to us
in the twenty-first century. But in the year AD 249, the emperor
Decius came up with a plan for re-energizing the empire—a
plan that included a return to traditional religion, that is, the
Greco-Roman gods. He apparently believed that the root cause
of the empire's decline was that the gods had been neglected,
and that the way to fix the problems of his society was to
appease the gods.

The one thing that stood in his way was the Church. Christianity was not simply one of the various religious options of
the time—not even just one among several movements toward
monotheism. Christians rejected the multiple gods of the
Greco-Roman pantheon, and refused to settle for consolidating them or worshipping a "high god" who reigned over the
other gods. Furthermore, Christianity was a religion based not
on the accident of birth or citizenship, but on personal faith
and free will choice. As such, the Church encouraged people
to convert from other belief systems, to leave their old gods
behind, and it required an exclusive relationship with the one
God of the Christians. And in spite of the high demands of
exclusive worship and moral accountability, people converted
and the Church grew. Many Jews were attracted to Christianity, in part because the Church did not require them to follow

the many laws of their ancestral faith.[7] Growing numbers of
Christians were refusing to participate in the practice of traditional Roman religion, in pagan worship—and this was happening at all levels of society and in every corner of the empire.
So it was that at this point in the history of the empire the
incompatibility of Christianity and Roman religion came to be
most clearly recognized.

Therefore, the emperor Decius decided to force the choice of
loyalty by requiring all inhabitants of the empire to make a sacrifice to the gods in his name. Those whose conscience would
not allow them to comply were tortured and/or executed.
Decius played on the average Roman's mistrust of Christians,
as well as the fear that if too many people stopped worshipping
the gods, tragic things would happen to the empire. The Christians came to be hated for what the Romans saw as "rigidity,"
or an inflexibility with regard to the worship of many gods.
Christians were called "atheists" because they acknowledged
only one God, and ironically the Roman establishment justified its intolerance for the Christian religion by calling the
Christians intolerant. This institutional intolerance had already
become imperial policy, but now, in the middle of the third
century, Decius used it to organize a full-scale, empire-wide
persecution of the Church. Half a century later, the emperor
Diocletian used a call to traditional religion as the rationale for
engaging in intensified persecution of the Church. Intolerance
of Christians came to a climax in what is generally known as
the Great Persecution, which lasted from about AD 303 to 313.

In spite of the persecution, the Church grew steadily
throughout its first three centuries, until there were some urban

areas with a Christian majority, and Christians could be found among the ranks of the poor and the rich, even in the imperial court. By the end of the fourth century, Christianity had become the official religion of the Roman Empire. So how did an illegal sect eventually succeed in converting the empire that had persecuted it? The answer is, in part, because Christians were willing to die rather than renounce their faith. Christians' embracing martyrdom, and also their willingness to risk death from illness while caring for the sick, impressed many pagans and convinced them to convert to the faith. That Christians were ready to risk their lives was evidence of their conviction that something greater than the present life was at stake. They had a bigger picture in mind, a life that is larger than life and extends beyond the present life; a life that is a gift from the God who is greater than the powers of this world. In his parables, Jesus told his disciples that the age of the Church would be an age of watching and waiting for something (Matthew 25:1–13)—something greater than any power or empire on earth. Therefore, Christians are willing to risk what they have now to gain what they hope for (Matthew 16:25; Mark 8:35; Luke 9:24).

The fourth century was a turning point in history for several reasons, not least of which is that the status of the Church changed dramatically when the emperor Constantine came to power and ended the persecution. He granted freedom of worship to all religions with the Edict of Milan in 313, finally legalizing Christianity.

Within the Church, it was in the fourth century that Christian monotheism was decisively defined. Of course monotheism was nothing new—the Christian version came from Judaism.

Some other cultures, such as the Egyptians, had approached it, though these forms of monotheism were arguably only a modified form of polytheism. The more intellectually minded among the Romans, led by the philosophers, were abandoning the old mythologies for the idea of one high god, with the other gods falling into place in a hierarchical pantheon of "principalities and powers." Although consolidating the countless gods would have been attractive to a lot of people, this high god was usually understood to be impersonal and so offered little comfort to people living a hard life. Other sects made movements toward monotheism, including some of the mystery cults, but these were in many ways imitations of Christianity, without the moral expectations.[8]

Christianity defined monotheism for Western culture. But which version of Christianity? As Constantine was annoyed to find out, there were competing interpretations within the Church, with schools of thought on the fringes that disagreed with the majority of the bishops precisely on the point of what it meant to believe in one God. The sticking point was the man, Jesus of Nazareth, called the Christ (which as most Christians know, means "the Anointed One"). As the central figure of the Christian faith, he was universally understood to be the Mediator and Reconciler of God and humanity. The problem was that there were alternative explanations of exactly how he was a mediator and what his relationship was with the one God. While the majority of the worldwide Church held that Jesus himself was divine, and therefore defined God as a Trinity that included God the Father, Jesus Christ, and the Holy Spirit, there were those who denied the Trinity, and counted

Christ among God's creatures. There is evidence that the
emperor Constantine had accepted a version of this nontrini-
tarian teaching at first, but he quickly (and quietly) changed
his understanding of God to be in line with those who upheld
the Church's established tradition. The details of these doctrinal controversies are beyond the scope of the present book. The
point for our purposes is that it was in the fourth century that
these debates came to a climax, and the outcome shaped the
definition of Christianity and in turn influenced what would
become a predominantly monotheistic culture.[9]

The Christian World

Thus in the fourth century, both the Church and the Roman
Empire were established in the course that they would follow
for as long as the empire continued to exist and beyond. But
what the emperor Constantine did in the early fourth century
was not what is commonly represented by those who seek to
criticize the Church's conversion of the empire; he did not
create a marriage of church and state. In the ancient world,
government and religion were interrelated, for the most part
because religion was a function of one's ethnicity. People
believed in the gods of their tribe or nation, which is to say the
gods of their ancestors. So when a tribe or nation went to war,
the outcome of battle was not thought to be decided by superior
numbers or weapons, but by superior deities. The people with
the more powerful god(s) won the war. We can see this kind
of thinking in the Old Testament. Many cultures believed that

their leaders were divinely appointed, and some of these leaders claimed that they were gods themselves. So the intimate
connection of religion and government is as old as civilization.

The personal faith of the emperor Constantine is a matter
of perpetual debate, and it is not necessary to try to settle the
matter here, except to say that whatever one believes about the
conversion of Constantine, he never ruled as a baptized Christian. Like many upwardly mobile men of his day, he postponed
his baptism (and the moral responsibilities that come with baptism) until the end of his life. He did claim to be a believer in
the one God of the Christians, and, what is more, he (perhaps
ironically) followed ancient precedent in claiming that he owed
his military success and his ascendency to the throne to God.
His support of the Church in the aftermath of the Great Persecution, going far above and beyond what could be thought
to be politically expedient, is evidence of the sincerity of his
faith. One of his first acts as emperor, even when he held only
the western half of the empire and still had not yet secured
the eastern half, was to issue the Edict of Milan in the year
313. With this edict, Constantine legalized Christianity, and
although he left no room for ambiguity on the matter of the
favored status of the Church, he did not establish Christianity
as the *only* legal religion of the empire.

The Edict of Milan did not outlaw paganism. In fact, it
promised tolerance and freedom of worship for all citizens of
the empire.[10] The end of the persecution of the Christians did
not mean that the tables were turned and the persecuted would
become the persecutors. On one level, Constantine could not
afford to alienate non-Christians. (Technically, the Edict of

Milan was issued along with the general Licinius, who was decidedly not Christian.) Although Constantine was not afraid to promote the interests of the Church, his overarching concern was the unity of the empire, and he needed the support of the pagans. But on another level, Constantine believed that faith had to come by free will, and that a forced conversion was no conversion at all. People must be free to be wrong, and to come to the truth in their own time.[11] After all, if God causes the sun to shine and the rain to fall on the righteous and unrighteous alike, then both righteous and unrighteous must be free to enjoy the benefits of the Pax Romana.

Therefore, putting an end to persecution of Christians would not be the reversal of persecution. Christians were encouraged to evangelize, but they were forbidden to retaliate. It is noteworthy that during all the time that they were being persecuted, Christians never took up arms against the authorities. And it must not go unnoticed that this nonconfrontational stance was ingrained not only in the Church's new converts, but also in the Church's most powerful convert, the emperor Constantine, and it was reflected in his political policies.[12] Constantine proclaimed that everyone should be allowed to live according to his or her own conscience, without fear.[13] Therefore, Constantine did not endorse forced conversions. Although he did make his pagan soldiers recite a generically monotheistic prayer while the Christian soldiers were at Mass, he did not force them to (pretend to) be converted or to be baptized. If the new emperor believed that God fought his battles for him, then surely God did not need the sword of Constantine to do God's work of converting souls. The bishop Athanasius of

Alexandria, a contemporary of Constantine, depicted the cross as an instrument of peace, an image that could be possible only during a time of religious tolerance.[14] The emperor Constantine's primary goal was unity, and he believed that unity—if it was going to be a peaceful existence—required a religious tolerance not previously known in the Roman Empire, or anywhere in the world for that matter.

Unfortunately, that vision of unity through tolerance was short-lived. After Constantine's death, his sons exacerbated the Church's internal conflicts over doctrine, and after their ambitions failed they left the empire in the hands of their relative, Julian -known to us as "the Apostate." Julian was one of the few survivors of a series of plots to whittle away rival heirs to the throne. He had gone to school with Saints Basil the Great and Gregory of Nazianzus, and even before their illustrious careers they suspected that he was secretly a pagan and held animosity toward the Church. When he became emperor in 361, he tried to discredit the Christian faith by reviving the mistrust and hatred of the days of Decius and Diocletian. He looked the other way when pagan factions rose up in anger against the Church, or pagan governors persecuted Christians in their provinces. He made it illegal for Christians to teach in Roman schools, and he allowed certain exiles to return to their home cities so that they could spread disunity and conflict within the churches. In short, his agenda (like that of Decius and Diocletian before him) was to bring back loyalty to the traditional gods, and, with that, to bring back the traditional religious intolerance of the Roman state. Embarrassed by the social outreach of the Church, he even tried (in vain) to replace its charitable work with a secular social welfare system that would be a form of social gospel without the Gospel.

As history (or providence) would have it, Julian's reign was also short-lived. Although his policies did not bring about a renewal of violent persecution of Christians, the cultural persecution that occurred was enough to frighten Julian's successors into taking a "never again" stance. The eventual result was exactly the kind of reversal Constantine had avoided. Theodosius I (r. 379–395) finally made paganism illegal (though this law seems not to have been enforced) and declared that trinitarian Christianity was the only legal religion of the empire through the Edict of Thessalonica in the year 380. This order established that even those versions of Christianity that were determined to be heretical were now against the law. With Theodosius, the empire had reverted to an alliance of government with religion, except that now the religion was Christianity. Trinitarian Christianity had won over paganism (and over heresy), but the Constantinian experiment of religious tolerance was over.

This was the shadow side of the victory of the Church over the empire. In a marriage of church and state, eventually religion becomes subordinated to government, and it can become a tool of the state. In the Roman Empire, religious tolerance was replaced by a state religion within a century of the Edict of Milan. This is the inherent danger of assuming that the government rules by divine appointment. Under this arrangement, any religious movement that does not support the government will inevitably be suspect. From there, the next step is the transition from a state religion to a religion of the state—in other

words, the state becomes the religion as religion itself is secu-
larized, reverting to civic duty rather than obedience to God.
From there, any religious movement that is perceived as upset-
ting the civic apple cart is treated as though it is antisocial, or
even treasonous.

John Lennon asked us to imagine a universe without
heaven, in other words, a world without religion. In doing so,
he was standing in the long tradition of thinkers like Edward
Gibbon, who proposed that religion was the real problem
behind all of society's ills. We would argue instead that religion is the solution to our problems, not the cause of them. But
for religion to solve problems, religion must promote the love
of neighbor and must allow the neighbor the freedom to follow
a different path (as long as that path also promotes the love of
neighbor). Therefore one important thing that the twenty-first
century must learn from the early Church is that the attempt to
force others to share one's views is at best counterproductive,
and in the end it is futile. Forced conversion dilutes the membership of any faith community, or, for that matter, any ideology. The integrity of any belief system demands that people
accept it by their own free will. As Saint Augustine lamented,
creating a situation in which people join begrudgingly, or for
reasons other than convictions about faith, only results in fill-
ing the group with false members.

Nevertheless, by the fourth century, the Christian Church
had overcome paganism, with its devaluation of human life and
dignity, and had converted an empire. As it did so, the Church
gave the world seven gifts that forever changed human culture. These seven gifts were the seven cultural revolutions that

have outlived both the persecuting empire and the converted empire, and in the end, they have shaped Western society (in fact most of the world) as we know it, and for the better. As we move forward into the near future, recognizing and reclaiming these gifts will become more important than ever.

The Post-Christian World

And so we fast-forward to our own time—the twenty-first century. Are there lessons that the Church of today (and tomorrow) can learn from the experiences and conclusions of the early Christians? We think there are, and for one very important reason. It has been said that our world is becoming a "post-Christian" world. This means that over the course of recent generations, there has been an observed decline in the Church's influence over society. Christianity is no longer the dominant religion in many places where it used to be, giving way to a secularist worldview under which more and more people are seeing religious faith and morality as not only optional and out-dated but even disagreeable.

The concept of morality can be difficult to define, precisely because of the relativism inherent in post-Christian culture. In other words, if we try to define what we mean by morality, it becomes too easy to dismiss the entire concept by asking, "Whose morality?" as though any system of ethics is as good as any other. But this posture negates morality. Rather, when we speak of morality, we are speaking of exactly the kinds of things that the seven revolutions changed in the world. We mean behavioral ethics that are based on the conviction that all people are created in the image of God, and no one is expendable; that individuals and the family must be protected from exploitation; and that people must be free to work and worship according to their own conscience.

In general, in a post-Christian culture the dominant worldview is no longer founded on Christian principles—or at least we can no longer assume that it will be. The Church no longer shapes the culture. But—and here's the point—in a very real sense, this "post-Christian" world is actually coming full circle to resemble the pre-Christian world—the world in which Christians were persecuted because they criticized the ethics of the culture and refused to participate in its idolatrous practices— practices that involved the exploitation of human beings. Therefore, the context of the Church in the world is moving increasingly toward what it was before the time of Constantine. This is true especially with regard to the place of religion in society, the values of the dominant culture, and popular conceptions of what is acceptable behavior. And although it may seem counterintuitive, given that the majority of people in the United States self-identify as Christians, the truth is that many self-proclaimed Christians are joining the paganization of the culture, not to mention the criticism of Christianity itself. Many Christian denominations in the United States are declining, as participation in a religious community comes to be seen as one optional affiliation among many. For many people, the Church has become a club that they may or may not choose to join (or which they may join but rarely participate in or support). By raising awareness of the culture's move toward post-Christianity, we are hoping that self-identifying Christians will accept the call to live according to the historical values of the Church, and to promote those values in the culture—something that the Catholic Church has called "The New Evangelization."

For the moment, one example will suffice to demonstrate how post-Christian culture is similar to pre-Christian. Like the Roman world, our culture is more and more enamored of entertainment that exploits other people. Real violence is available for viewing in our own homes, not just the gladiator-like "ultimate fighting," but also the reality police shows and the televised murder trials, complete with gory photographs.[15] It is understandable that we are curious about tragic events and that we wish at times to escape from the drama (or boredom) of our own lives by indulging in the drama of other people's lives. But we have to be very careful that we don't become voyeurs as we revel in the real personal heartache and embarrassment of people played out on "reality TV." We watch people humiliate themselves, and in watching we participate in the loss of their human dignity.

In Roman society this kind of glorification of humiliation and violence contributed to people's desensitization to suffering, pain, and death, and the same thing is happening now in our own culture. Desensitization, in turn, leads to dehumanization, especially of the weak. We are not talking about fiction, action films, or even video games, but about actual televised violence and humiliation.[16] Watching these troublesome scenes, sometimes even as they happen, and treating them as entertainment, contributes to a new kind of stoicism, which is to say a lack of empathy caused by the buffer of technology.

In other words, when people see traumatic things on a screen, they can tend to dismiss the pain, and indeed the very humanity, of those who are experiencing the painful episodes that are being recorded and disseminated.

The Church of the twenty-first century will have to take a stand against the marginalization of religion and the dehumanization of those who are exploited in the name of entertainment. But in doing so the Church will become fair game for ridicule. Just as the Church was once criticized for being antisocial—for rejecting some of the cultural elements the Roman people held most dear—the contemporary Church will once again be criticized for refusing to affirm the "rights" and the "choice" of modern secular society, and indeed this is already happening. It has come to the point where even those who choose to have large families are often ridiculed and called irresponsible, as though they should naturally share a value that says more children are a burden on society, and they should naturally want to prevent children from being born.

It used to be that devotion to God was respected, even by those who did not practice religious faith. In Western society, Christian clergy were treated with respect, even by those who did not accept the faith. The collar meant something. Just watch a few old movies and you'll see how clergy were once in a category with police officers and teachers—they were seen as people who could be trusted. Admittedly, some of the erosion of respect for clergy is owing to the small number of clergy who have abused their position, and this reaction is understandable. Yet it is now commonplace to assume that aberrant clergy are the rule rather than the exception, to the point where it has become

acceptable to take every opportunity to criticize religion and religious leaders. But to blame the Christian religion for the failures of a few of its leaders is illogical, and to reject the teachings
of Jesus (not to mention the forgiveness and reconciliation with
God that he offers) because some of his followers have abused
their power is to punish yourself for the sins of another. Yet
many people have done just that. And many have attempted to
replace the Church with something else—often something hu-
manitarian, but ultimately something very secular. As we will
discuss in the following chapters, the emerging religion of the
current empire is a secular religion, one very much like the civic
religion of the Roman Empire—one in which people value their
freedom to indulge in whatever they please but will compromise
religious freedom if they perceive that religious people might
critique or curtail their personal freedom.

We want to be clear that the point here is not to compare the
United States to the Roman Empire. That has been done, with
varying degrees of success.[17] The point is to highlight the simi-
larities between the pre-Christian world (the world before the
legalization of Christianity and the conversion of the world) and
the new post-Christian world, because both the pre-Christian
world and the post-Christian world are anti-Christian.[18] The values of both the pre-Christian and the post-Christian world are
different from Christian values, and that difference makes the
Christian lifestyle stand out; that difference makes Christians
the target of criticism by those who perceive Christian values as
being a threat to their understanding of personal freedom. To
be sure, in American culture, even in a post-Christian world,
persecution of the Church has so far been nonviolent.[19] Rather, it

will be more subtle—what might be called cultural persecution.
Nevertheless, the choice of loyalty to Christ versus Caesar (that
is, Christ versus culture) is being confronted again, in some of
the same ways it once was, and in some new ways.

Increasingly, Christians must live as cultural salmon, swim-
ming upstream, and branded with labels such as unenlightened,
closed-minded, and rigid—labels that are being used to marginalize the faithful. Such is the hypocrisy of ultra-tolerance.
In a world where it is politically correct to preach tolerance for
all, tradition seems to be exempt from that so-called tolerance.
Tradition and traditional values, which are perceived to threaten
the absolute freedoms of some, are simply labeled intolerant,
and then they no longer need to be tolerated. The irony is that at
times it seems as if the only sin left is to claim that something is
a sin. But Jesus said, "Blessed are you when they insult you and
persecute you and utter every kind of evil against you [falsely]
because of me. Rejoice and be glad, for your reward will be great
in heaven. Thus they persecuted the prophets (martyrs) who
were before you" (Matthew 5:11–12, NAB).

Having said all of that, our goal is not to point fingers and
breed more distrust. Our aim in this book is not to draw a line
in the sand. The last thing the world needs is more "us versus them" rhetoric. Christians are called to convert the world,
not make an enemy of it; we are to promote reconciliation not
division. The Church must model the tolerance that the world
refuses to grant, even to the point of being tolerant of those
who choose to be nonreligious. However, when secularism
becomes a religion, as it has in our own time, the criticism that
Christians are unenlightened cannot be allowed to be used to

bully the religious into conformity with a secular ideology. In other words, tolerance must work both ways, and the charge of intolerance must not be used to justify intolerance.

As we move more and more into a post-Christian world, the solution we will propose is that we follow the example of the early Christians, who had never known a world in which Christianity was aligned with the dominant culture or had such a great influence. So we are not trying to foster animosity; we are trying to promote participation in the work of God in the world. Ironically, as that work becomes more difficult in a world that refuses to follow the lead of the Church, the work will become more clear because it will stand out in contrast with the culture.

Gone are the days when it was fashionable, or even acceptable, to be a Christian. In spite of the fact that a majority of people in First World countries self-identify as Christian, many of these self-proclaimed Christians are joining in the Church bashing. Those who embrace the values of their faith in a world where doing so is frowned upon are the ones who will witness by their very example. And people will see that they are willing to risk the comforts of conformity for the sake of something bigger—a life bigger than life—the kingdom of God.

The Seven Revolutions

So how can the Church live and serve in this new post-Christian world, in which believers are facing various forms of persecution? The starting place is to look at the Church as it existed in the pre-Christian world, and to look at the seven revolutions—the seven ways that the Church changed the world—the seven gifts that the Church gave the world, which affected human relationships in ever widening concentric circles.

In the realm of the individual (Chapter 2), the Church revolutionized the way society defined personhood. To affirm the universal dignity of human life requires the strong to speak up for and defend the weak, those who can't speak for themselves. In the ancient world, for some people the ability to speak was the very litmus test of humanity. Those who could not speak (babies) or those who could not speak the languages of civilization (the "barbarians," who did not speak Greek or Latin) were considered less than fully human and were denied the benefits of society. One Roman writer said that as long as they cannot talk, babies were more like vegetables than like human beings. Yet from the very beginning, the Church affirmed the value of all human life and resisted exploitation and dehumanization. Because of the Christians, this way of looking at humanity became so much a part of Western culture that eventually the Constitution of the United States would be built around the concept that all people are created equal (though this stipulation would not be applied to everyone at first). Long before the Constitution was applied equally to all people in this country, the Catholic Church had already condemned abortion, the abuse of children, and slavery.

In the realm of the home (Chapter 3), the Church revolutionized the way the world saw the family. The foundational value of personhood was applied with equity to women and even to children.[20] And, more important, with the development of the Church, the exploitation of all those who lacked support systems was rejected and critiqued. In the realm of what we might call the workplace (Chapter 4), Christianity emphasized the dignity of human labor. Based on the assumed value of the individual person, the Church affirmed the honor in manual labor and eventually rid the world of the belief that one person could own another. In the realm of religion (Chapter 5), the Church defined itself, and, by extension, religion in general. Christianity redefined what it meant for humanity to connect with the Divine and in the process it taught that God is love, and union with God is open to all humans. Thus the Church recognized, in the course of its struggle to define itself, the importance of inclusiveness and the value of unity.

In the realm of the community (Chapter 6), Christians looked outward from the Church and cared for the poor and the sick, regardless of their religion. The concept of Christian charity was something alien to the self-centered perspective of Roman culture, yet by the end of the fourth century Christian charity had replaced Greco-Roman virtue as the goal of human progress.

In the realm of ultimate concerns, Christianity influenced attitudes toward life and death (Chapter 7), not to mention belief in the afterlife. And by doing so, Christians further promoted a culture of life. This new culture of life (and eternal life) gave people the hope they desperately needed, which led to the freedom to rise above the daily grind, and even to express their God-given creativity through art. Finally, in the realm of the state (Chapter 8), the Church revolutionized government. Beginning with Constantine, emperors admitted not only that they were not gods, but also that they were not above the law, and that they were morally accountable to God. Although some, like

Constantine, considered the postponement of baptism a loop-
hole in the system, the fact that he thought he had to postpone
his baptism to avoid accountability proves the point. There was
a higher power, an authority over the emperor, one who had behavioral expectations for the emperor, and one who could remove the emperor from the throne if he did not measure up.
With all of these seven revolutions in mind, it is indeed remarkable that the Church, born of oppression in the Roman Empire,
would be the entity that brought hope to the world.

It is true that there have been times throughout its history
when the Church forgot some of the lessons it had learned—
the shadow side of the alliance with empires resulted in the
endorsement of the subjugation of native peoples, forced conversions, and other forms of coercion and oppression. But these
mistakes only highlight the need for the contemporary Church
to reclaim its original convictions. Once we have discussed the
seven revolutions in detail, the last two chapters will demonstrate why reclaiming these revolutions is so important for the
Church of the twenty-first century. Chapter 9 will take in the
big picture, the relevance of the early Church for the Church of
the future, and Chapter 10 will offer some concrete suggestions
for taking action in the new post-Christian world.

Christians can influence the world for the better again. But
it will mean making a commitment to stand by a worldview that
current society often rejects and ridicules. It will mean making a commitment to accept a countercultural position in society, while many who call themselves Christian simply allow
themselves to be converted by the culture. It will mean waking
up to the reality of cultural persecution (as well as the violent

persecution still going on in many countries) and resisting it. As we have noted, this cultural persecution may be subtle, and it may take the form of pressure from areas as diverse as marketing media, with its temptations toward materialism, and education, with its skepticism about anything spiritual or miraculous. Christians will need to recognize these challenges to traditional faith, call them out, and resist them. We will also need to support one another when we do this, speaking up for our brothers and sisters when they are ridiculed—even if it's just for giving thanks to God when they accept an award or make a touchdown. In this way, the Church of the twenty-first century can overcome the new paganism the way the Church of the pre-Christian world overcame the old paganism—that is, by refusing to deny the faith and by being willing to risk our lives (or the comfort of our lifestyles) for something bigger than life.

Chapter 2

A REVOLUTION OF THE PERSON

The Invention of Human Dignity

"We are equally forbidden," wrote Tertullian, "to wish ill, to do ill, to speak ill, to think ill of everyone. The thing we must not do to an emperor, we must not do to anyone else."[1]

A respected jurist in North Africa, Tertullian knew the weight of every word he wrote. He composed his great defense of Christian faith, his *Apologeticum,* as a response to wild rumors that were common in the second century—that Christians practiced ritual cannibalism, that they held orgies in their churches, that they routinely committed incest. These charges were the stuff of whisper campaigns, and they made it easy for governors to justify persecution to an anxious populace. Christians, they believed, must be suppressed because they were perverse and dangerous.

Today, Tertullian's words read as harmless democratic clichés about equality. They reflect truths that much of the world has come to accept as self-evident. *Of course,* citizens and rulers are created equal; and *of course* they share basic rights; and *of course* they are both parties to a social contract between governors and the governed.

But none of these principles were self-evident in Tertullian's world; and his words, in AD 197 in the city of Carthage, would have struck aristocrats as revolutionary and dangerous.

There was no idea of "equality" in that world. Things were very different for the rich and powerful—the 1 percent, as we might call them today. The 99 percent were their toys, legally speaking. The pagan world had no notion of "human rights"—no idea that a human being was a person who was somehow sacred just because they were human. So life could be pretty miserable for those ordinary millions.

But in a different way, life was even more miserable for the 1 percent. The richest and most educated—like the emperor Marcus Aurelius—were dabbling in philosophies that promised a way out of the misery of the real world. They seemed to have everything; yet they were looking for an escape.

Then Christians arrived with their strange ideas. In a way the pagans were right: Christians—as Tertullian argued—were shaking up the social order. The ways of the Christians would prove to be revolutionary.

The Few and the Many

Today, when anyone wants to plead their case to the media, they appeal to certain notions they consider to be self-evident: that all people have equal standing. They often ask special treatment based on their "victimhood," as if victimhood conferred a certain dignity. They assume, too, that there is no right of the stronger to dominate the weaker. The ACLU will tell you that laws exist to protect the weak. Where did that idea come from?

Such a notion, and many other similar notions, would have struck thinking pagans as absurd. You won't find them defended in the writings of Aristotle or Cicero. In pagan culture, no preferential treatment was due to victims. There was no duty to protect the weak. Victims were losers, and equality was an absurdity. Even Athenian democracy excluded most of the population, and Athenian democracy was itself an aberration in the ancient world. As the historian Thucydides put it: "the strong do as they wish, and the weak suffer what they must."[2]

Then where did these ideas of equal rights, of the dignity of victims, of protection of the weak, come from? They came from Jesus Christ. They were propagated by his Church. And they were announced within a world that was pervasively mean, callous, hopeless, and loveless.

It takes a real effort of the imagination for us to see the world the way it was in ancient Rome. We have to abandon all our notions of equal rights under the law. In that day and age, there was only a small minority who had rights—the Roman citizens.

These days, in almost any country, whoever is born in that country is a "citizen" of that country, and the poorest citizen theoretically has the same legal rights as the wealthiest citizen. But in the Roman Empire, citizens were a privileged minority. Saint Paul was one of them, and more than once he used his Roman citizenship to good effect.

And as they cried out and waved their garments and threw dust into the air, the tribune commanded him to be brought into the barracks, and ordered him to be examined by scourging, to find out why they shouted thus against him.

But when they had tied him up with the thongs, Paul said to the centurion who was standing by, "Is it lawful for you to scourge a man who is a Roman citizen, and uncondemned?"

When the centurion heard that, he went to the tribune and said to him, "What are you about to do? For this man is a Roman citizen."

So the tribune came and said to him, "Tell me, are you a Roman citizen?"

And he said, "Yes."

The tribune answered, "I bought this citizenship for a large sum."

Paul said, "But I was born a citizen."

So those who were about to examine him withdrew from him instantly; and the tribune also was afraid, for he realized that Paul was a Roman citizen and that he had bound him.

—Acts 22:23–29

This happened in Jerusalem, where Paul had been the center of a near riot. As this little story shows us, it was illegal for a government official to torture a Roman citizen without a trial. But it was just fine for him to torture someone who wasn't a Roman citizen, guilty or not, just on the off chance that the torture might reveal some information. And the natural assumption was that any random person wandering the streets of

Jerusalem was not a Roman citizen. It was so unusual for someone to be a Roman citizen there, in fact, that the tribune had not
even considered the possibility. He didn't bother to ask.

Human rights? The idea would have made no sense if you
had tried to explain it. Why would you have "rights" just
because you were born? You had rights if you were somebody
important—like Paul, the son of a citizen. Or you could have
rights if you bought them, as the tribune had. But ordinary
people didn't have rights. The people existed for the state, and
if they were not useful to the state they had no right to exist.

And those are the ordinary "free" people we're talking
about. We haven't even mentioned the millions of slaves. In
some districts, slaves made up more than half the population.

So the pagan Roman Empire was divided between the very
few, who had wealth and privileges, and the great many, who
had nothing at all, legally speaking. The wealthy could live
lives of idle dissipation; the many struggled to live at all.

Roman society placed little value on the individual lives of
the "many." The average free Roman's idea of a good time was to
go watch the "shows"—lavish entertainments in which profes-
sional murderers killed one another in front of cheering throngs
of thousands. The death of gladiators was simply entertainment.

A "Sexual Paradise"

Such gross inequalities made for strange, and brutal, bedfel-
lows—though even the best scholars do not always show us the
brutality.

In his popular history of antiquity, the historian Norman Cantor praises the ancient empire because, he says, it "was very far from imposing sexual repression. Divorce was easy," he adds. "Prostitution flourished without controls. Homosexuality was commonplace. Even bestiality was practiced and received little censure. . . . The Roman Empire was," he concludes, ". . . a sexual paradise."[3]

A sexual paradise! Well, let's think about that.

If it was a paradise, it was "paradise" for only the 1 percent—the privileged classes who, when they weren't murdering one another, could afford to indulge every whim. They had slaves to rape whenever they liked, and since a slave was property, he or she just had to take it. Slaves made up at least a third of the population of ancient Italy—and about half of them were owned by the 1 percent, the richest of the rich.

But was life even paradise for the 1 percent? If we look at the effects of their lifestyle, it seems that the rich and powerful were miserable in spite of their material comforts. The cleverest among them were looking to the Stoic philosophy as their escape route: complete detachment from the world was the only way to avoid misery—one hardly dared speak of achieving happiness. And what's even more striking is that the upper classes simply stopped procreating. Norman Cantor's sexual paradise was a society that couldn't bring itself to wish its life on another generation. As we'll soon see, the demographic decline of the Roman upper classes was a constant worry to the most enlightened emperors—but their most cleverly devised legislation could do nothing to halt it. The emperor might be a philosopher-king with the most exalted ideas about friendship and duty, but the citizens of this paradise couldn't think of anything or anyone worthy of the smallest sacrifice of their convenience. They were incapable of sacrifice, and so they were incapable of love. They were devoid of hope.

For Christians, Norman Cantor's idea of paradise is their idea of hell. Remember the motto at the entrance to Dante's hell: *Abandon hope all you who enter.* And these people *had* abandoned hope. If they were living in paradise, why were they so miserable?

They were miserable because they were living in "a world without love," as one famous historian put it.[4]

A world without love was a miserable place for anyone, rich or poor. The bloody horror of life in the pagan world was a frequent theme of early Christian writers, who lived in that world but saw it with clearer eyes. Saint Cyprian, for example, sounds astoundingly modern as he condemns war, crime, and the gladiators:

> For a brief space imagine yourself to be transported to one of the loftiest peaks of some inaccessible mountain. From there, gaze on the appearances of things lying below you, and with eyes turned in various directions look upon the eddies of the billowy world, while you yourself are removed from earthly contacts. You will at once begin to feel compassion for the world, and with self-recollection and increasing gratitude to God, you will rejoice with all the greater joy that you have escaped it. Consider the roads blocked up by robbers, the seas beset with pirates, wars scattered all over the earth with the bloody horror

of camps. The whole world is wet with mutual blood; and murder, which in the case of an individual is admitted to be a crime, is called a virtue when it is committed wholesale. Impunity is claimed for the wicked deeds, not on the plea that they are guiltless, but because the cruelty is perpetrated on a grand scale.

And now, if you turn your eyes and your regards to the cities themselves, you will behold a concourse more fraught with sadness than any solitude. The gladiatorial games are prepared, that blood may gladden the lust of cruel eyes. The body is fed up with stronger food, and the vigorous mass of limbs is enriched with brawn and muscle, that the wretch fattened for punishment may die a harder death. Man is slaughtered that man may be gratified, and the skill that is best able to kill is an exercise and an art. Crime is not only committed, but it is taught. What can be said more inhuman or more repulsive? Training is undergone to acquire the power to murder, and the achievement of murder is its glory.

What state of things, I pray you, can that be, and what can it be like, in which men, whom none have condemned, offer themselves to the wild beasts—men of ripe age, of sufficiently beautiful person, clad in costly garments? Living men, they are adorned for a voluntary death; wretched men, they boast of their own miseries. They fight with beasts, not for their crime, but for their madness. Fathers look on their own sons; a brother is in the arena, and his sister is hard by; and although a

grander display of pomp increases the price of the exhibi-
tion, yet, oh shame! even the mother will pay the increase
in order that she may be present at her own miseries.
And in looking upon scenes so frightful and so impious
and so deadly, they do not seem to be aware that they are
parricides with their eyes.[5]

There, in a particularly vivid and imaginative description, we see exactly what a world without love is like. The gladiator is degraded by his work; and by means of his work he degrades great crowds of onlookers, including his own parents and siblings. Crime is called virtue in such a world, and power is license to maim and kill.

The Utility of Life

We don't mean that pagans never felt love for one another. Like all human beings, they felt strong attachments to family, to lovers, and to friends. They wrote beautiful tributes to friendship, the bond between equals that made them one soul. Some pagans loved their husbands or wives, although the popular literature of the day sneered at them for doing so. Roman comedies are more likely to show marriage as an intolerable burden.

Look here, father. Do you love my mother?
Love her? I? I love her now for not being near.
And when she is near?
I yearn for a death in the family.[6]

Even when there was personal love, there was no *charity*—no universal love for all. An educated pagan loved the people it was reasonable to love. There could be love between friends, and there could be friendship between equals. There could be love for one's family, but that was subject to the laws of reason. One shouldn't take it to extremes.

What is striking about pagan attitudes toward the family is just how reasonable they were. It was reason gone mad. If you want to see just how little the pagan world thought of human life, you'll find pagan attitudes in their starkest form in what the best minds in the world had to say about children.

Pagan philosophers were big on eugenics, to use a term that became popular in the nineteenth century. They thought humans should be bred as carefully as we breed cattle. And they thought the children born of those carefully planned unions should be brought up primarily to be useful.

Utility was the key factor in deciding whether a human being was worthy of living. The useful should be rewarded, and the useless should be thrown away.

When the Good News was new, abortion and even infanticide were commonplace in the culture, requiring little deliberation. In all of history, only one culture had forbidden these practices—that of the Jews. And they were an insignificant minority in the first century, mostly exiled from their homeland, especially after the disastrous rebellion that led to the destruction of Jerusalem in the year 70.

Every other nation, every other empire, every other kingdom, every other people—the Assyrians, the Babylonians, the Hittites, the Greeks, the Romans—routinely killed their young.

Plato and Aristotle commended abortion and infanticide. As the philosopher Seneca said, getting rid of useless children was simply the reasonable thing to do.

> *We knock mad dogs on the head, we slaughter fierce and savage bulls, and we doom scabby sheep to the knife, lest they should infect our flocks: we destroy monstrous births, and we also drown our children if they are born weakly or unnaturally formed; to separate what is useless from what is sound is an act, not of anger, but of reason.*[7]

The decision wasn't even up for debate. To dissent from this practice seemed as outlandish as refusing to use electricity seems today. Killing babies was just what people did and what everyone had always done, through all recorded history.

Plato, in his *Republic,* has his master Socrates work out the business of child rearing pretty thoroughly. When men and women have children, those children are born for the state. And the state has a strong interest in having the best possible children. Therefore children should be born of parents who are in peak physical condition.

SOCRATES: We said, you remember, that the children ought to be the issue of parents who are still in their prime.

GLAUCON: True.

SOCRATES: And do you agree with me that the prime of life may be reasonably reckoned at a period of twenty years for a woman, and thirty for a man?

GLAUCON: Where do you place these years?

SOCRATES: I should make it the rule for a woman
    to bear children to the state from her twentieth
    to her fortieth year: and for a man, after getting
    over the sharpest burst in the race of life, thence-
    forward to beget children to the state until he is
    fifty-five years old.

GLAUCON: Doubtless, he said, in both sexes, this
    is the period of their prime, both of body and
    mind.

So men and women ought to be of the right age for bearing
children. And Socrates has already decided that the state will
determine the circumstances under which they reproduce, so
as to breed the best possible citizens for the state.

But what happens to children who don't meet his criteria?

SOCRATES: But as soon as the women and the men
    are past the prescribed age, we shall allow the
    latter, I imagine, to associate freely with whom-
    soever they please, so that it be not a daughter,
    or mother, or daughter's child, or grandmother;
    and in like manner we shall permit the women
    to associate with any man, except a son or a
    father, or one of their relations in the direct line,
    ascending or descending; but only after giving
    them strict orders to do their best, if possible,
    to prevent any child, haply so conceived, from
    seeing the light, but if that cannot sometimes

be helped, to dispose of the infant on the understanding that the fruit of such a union is not to
be reared.[8]

Once they're past their prime childbearing years, men and
women can be as promiscuous as they like. They just have to
understand that if any children happen to be conceived through
their frolicking, those children will not be up to standard and
will have to be thrown away. Abortion is preferable, but infanticide will do if abortion doesn't work.

Aristotle, the other big name in classical philosophy, found
plenty to disagree with in Plato. But on the subject of rearing
fit citizens for the state, the two were mostly in agreement—
although we might note that Plato would have women educated in the same way as men, whereas Aristotle preferred his
women toned and physically fit but stupid:

> *Women who are with child should be careful of them-
> selves; they should take exercise and have a nourishing
> diet. The first of these prescriptions the legislator will
> easily carry into effect by requiring that they shall take
> a walk daily to some temple, where they can worship
> the gods who preside over birth. Their minds, however,
> unlike their bodies, they ought to keep unexercised, for
> the offspring derive their natures from their mothers as
> plants do from the earth.*

At the very least, women should be stupid enough to fall for
that daily-walk law.

Aristotle agreed with Plato that the state had no interest in maintaining children who were not fit. And if the state had no interest in them, then the state must throw them away.

> *As to the exposure and rearing of children, let there be a law that no deformed child shall live, but where there are too many (for in our state population has a limit), when couples have children in excess, and the state of feeling is averse to the exposure of offspring, let abortion be procured before sense and life have begun; what may or may not be lawfully done in these cases depends on the question of life and sensation.*[9]

It's interesting to notice that Aristotle takes into account public outrage against infanticide. Apparently outrage was possible in his time. He's practical: obviously "exposure" (leaving the babies out to die) would be the reasonable thing to do, but there might be laws or traditions against it. It's important to take those into account and abort while there's time.

Criteria for Personhood

By the time the Roman Empire had surrounded the Mediterranean, that "irrational" prejudice against infanticide had disappeared.

At Oxyrhynchus in Egypt, not long ago, there emerged a letter with the sublimely symbolic date of 1 BC. A pagan businessman named Hilarion was writing home to his pregnant wife, Alis. Amid the usual endearments, he says: "If you are delivered of a child [before I come home], if it is a boy, keep it, if a girl discard it."[10]

If it is a girl, discard it. A girl was a burden on her father. She could not get a job and contribute to the family's wealth; instead she represented a colossal expense, because she would require a dowry once she was of a marriageable age. The Roman playwrights referred to female offspring as "odious daughters."[11]

Daughters were costly. That was why families usually married off a girl at age eleven, to a much older man not of her choosing, thereby moving her off the books, off the dole. But many girls—in some places most of them—never lived to that age, because they were killed off at birth. This wasn't a crime. Even to kill an older child, as punishment, was a parent's legal right in Rome. Killing a newborn was a matter of no consequence whatsoever.

In Rome, a child did not achieve personhood until they were recognized by the head of the family, the father. When the mother had given birth, a midwife placed the child on the floor and summoned the father into the room. He examined the child with his criteria of selection in mind.

Was the child his? If the man suspected his wife of adultery, he might reject the child without so much as a glance.

If the child was an "odious daughter," he would likely turn on his heel and leave the room.

If the child was "defective" in any way, he would do the

same. Remember Seneca's adage: *What is good must be set apart from what is good-for-nothing.*

Life or death? It all depended on the will of a man. Human life began when the child was accepted into society. A man did not "have a child." He "took a child." The father "raised up" the child by picking it up from the floor.

The nonpersons who were left on the floor—while their mothers watched from a birthing chair—would be drowned immediately in a bucket of water, or brought to the town dump to be exposed to wild dogs and vultures. If they survived for any considerable time there, they might be rescued by pimps and raised up as child prostitutes. It was all legal and above board. It was the *right thing to do,* as any reasonable and well-adjusted pagan philosopher would tell you.

How often did this happen? It happened in most families. In cities, it happened every day. It's not only in the documentary record—like the businessman's letters home—it's in the archaeological record. Archaeologists have unearthed vast dumps of infant corpses from the Roman period, in places as distant as Ashkelon (in present-day Israel) and Scotland. In Ashkelon an ancient sewer was found clogged with the bones of newborns, presumably most of them female.

We have the census records from ancient Delphi, where we see that out of six hundred families only *six* raised more than one daughter.[12] *Many* families had multiple sons. Only *1 percent* had multiple daughters. Where did all those girls go? Into the sewer. Out to the town dump.

They were of no use in the Roman world. They had no

personhood. In the ancient languages, they would say they had no face.[13] No rights. No protection before the law. No standing in the philosophy that undergirded the law.

This was what Roman family values looked like.

Christians and Killing

When the Christians came along, they brought completely alien ideas that threatened to overturn everything the Romans believed about the family, because Christians had completely different assumptions about what it meant to be a person.

In Roman culture at the time of the early Church, the father had absolute control over every member of his family—including power over life and death. Under the Roman Republic, a paterfamilias—the head of a household—could legally execute his son if he thought that the son deserved it. And the father alone determined whether the son deserved it. Christian teachings held that human life was sacred. The fact that God had created each individual meant that the father's power was not absolute. "Honor your father and your mother," yes (and even those words "and your mother" were an assault on Roman family values), but "You shall not kill" above all.

"You shall not kill" was an idea that had to be explained to educated Romans, who had no notion that human life was sacred just because it was human. Refuting the common accusation that Christians were secret cannibals (because the Romans knew they simply had to be up to *something*), Saint

Athenagoras explained that Christians could never be murderers, because they refused even to kill an unborn child. They refused to *watch* the gladiatorial games, because they thought that enjoying watching gladiators being murdered was the same as participating in the murdering themselves:

> *If that is what our character is like, then what man of sound mind will affirm that we are murderers? For we cannot eat human flesh till we have killed someone. The former charge, therefore, being false, if any one should ask them in regard to the second, whether they have seen what they assert, not one of them would be so barefaced as to say that he had. And yet we have slaves, some more and some fewer, by whom we could not help being seen; but even of these, not one has been found to invent even such things against us.*
>
> *For when they know that we cannot endure even to see a man put to death, though justly, who of them can accuse us of murder or cannibalism? Who does not reckon among the things of greatest interest the contests of gladiators and wild beasts—especially those which are given by you [the emperor, whose gladiatorial entertainments were proportionately lavish]? But we, deeming that to see a man put to death is much the same as killing him, have abjured such spectacles. How, then, when we do not even look on, lest we should contract guilt and pollution, can we put people to death?*
>
> *And when we say that those women who use drugs to bring on abortion commit murder, and will have to give*

an account to God for the abortion, on what principle
should we commit murder? The same person could not
regard the very fetus in the womb as a created being, and
therefore an object of God's care—and then kill it when
it has passed into life. The same person could not refuse
to expose an infant, because those who expose them are
chargeable with child-murder, and on the other hand,
destroy it when it has been brought up. But we are in all
things always alike and the same, submitting ourselves
to reason, and not ruling over it.[14]

Killing was a "normal" part of family life in ancient Rome, an unsurprising final act in an afternoon's entertainment at the circus. But Athenagoras, like the other Christian apologists of the second century, said that such events were opposed to Christian principle and could never be assimilated as "normal" in a Christian life.

A Consistent Christian Ethic

These are not isolated cases of Christians harboring what were seen at the time as strange ideas. Athenagoras was speaking for the whole Church. Abortion was condemned in the first century in the Christian manual called the *Didache* and in the *Epistle of Barnabas;* in the second century in the *Apocalypse of Peter* and by Saint Justin Martyr, Saint Clement of Alexandria, Tertullian of Carthage, Minucius Felix in Italy, and Hippolytus in Rome; and in the third century by Origen of Alexandria,

Saint Cyprian of Carthage, and many others. The condemnation has been consistent through time, and universal in the Church—from Africa and Asia through all of Europe.

The *Didache* is the earliest extrabiblical document that has survived, and it begins with these words: "Two Ways there are, one of Life and one of Death, and there is a great difference between the Two Ways."

Around the year AD 155, Saint Justin Martyr wrote to the emperor: "We have been taught that it is wicked to expose even newly born children. . . . For we would then be murderers."[15] We've already heard Athenagoras, from about the same time, say the same thing.

These were the strange ideas that Christians were forcing the Roman world to face for the first time—sticks of dynamite planted at the base of the Romans' assumptions about the world. In a world that tolerated only the useful, Christians demanded protection for the most vulnerable and "useless" persons. The early Christians created the first truly tolerant, welcoming, and all-inclusive society—with a remarkable social welfare system, even from the very beginning.

> *And all who believed were together and had all things in common; and they sold their possessions and goods and distributed them to all, as any had need. (Acts 2:44-45)*

Christians not only tolerated the poor and weak; they loved them with a human affection. They saw the least members of the human family as images of God, as other Christs who must be welcomed, as angels requiring hospitality. They saw every human being as a person.

"Widows and orphans are to be revered like the altar."[16] That's what the third-century *Didascalia Apostolorum* proclaimed, and it was what Christians believed. In the ancient world, widows and orphans were among the faceless poor. To Christians they were like the Holy Eucharist.

From such reverence for life came true social security, true stability and prosperity. And we have some very interesting evidence of the difference Christianity made in the lives of some individual children.

What's in a Name?

Not long ago, Italian archaeologists completed an exhaustive survey of all the inscriptions and graffiti in the Roman catacombs.[17] One portion of the study dealt with the names bestowed and taken by the Christians who lived in Rome. How many took biblical names? How many were named after early martyrs? How many Christian parents stuck with the old, traditional Roman names?

An illuminating subsection covers "Humiliating names or nicknames." There we learn that some Christians chose to bear names like *Proiectus,* which means "cast off" or "thrown away like trash." Others went through life with the Roman name *Stercorius* or the Greek *Coprion.* These names are hard to translate in polite company, but they are vulgar terms for human waste—excrement. Why would Christians choose to bear such names? It's likely that those particular Romans were, as infants, rescued from the dung heap—rescued by Christians from the place where Romans abandoned "defective" or female new-borns. They had been exposed there, like trash, to die quickly from the elements or be attacked by the claws of scavenging beasts.

Proiectus, Stercorius, Coprion—all of these people were lucky to be alive, but as children they must have had to suffer the taunts of playmates, who were pleased to remind them of their lowly origins. Who's your daddy? Your daddy is the dung heap. Your name is trash.

Those who were rescued by Christians could, at the time of their baptism, choose any new name they wished: Matthew, Mark, Mary, or Martha. Yet a goodly number of them chose to hold on to those insulting names. Saint Hilary, in the fourth century, names a Stercorius among his fellow bishops![18]

Historians believe that Christians kept their foul nicknames as an act of humility—or perhaps triumphant irony. These children who were dung in the eyes of imperial Rome knew that they were precious in the sight of God. Just by virtue of having been created in the image of God, they were *persons,* with as much right to live as the richest senator in Rome.

A helpless child is a person. A blind widow is a person. A crippled slave is a person. This awareness was a revolutionary change that Christianity brought to the world, and all the other revolutions depend on this one.

CHAPTER 3

A REVOLUTION IN THE HOME

The New Idea of Family

C hristians saw each individual person as uniquely valuable. But people are meant to live together in larger units. "It is not good that the man should be alone" (Genesis 2:18). We're meant to live our lives together, and the most fundamental unit of togetherness is the family.

What is a family?

This is a simple question that we don't ask very often because we know the answer. We see all kinds of broken families in our world, but we know they're broken because they don't match our idea of what a family is supposed to be. A family is a group of related people who live together in a loving relationship. Father, mother, and children are the core of the family.

We know what the ideal family is, even in a world where so many families are broken and scattered. The nuclear family may be more the exception than the rule in real life, but it is the ideal—the answer we automatically give to "What is a family?"

But that simple answer is a Christian answer. The pagan answer was vastly different. In pagan times, a family was a man— the paterfamilias, or father of the family—and his property.

Love is seldom part of the vocabulary when pagans talk

about the family. They speak of duty but not love. The pagan family was the smallest unit of the state, and it was really more a form of government than a relationship of love.

Christians and pagans agreed that human beings were social creatures: "Man is a political animal," Aristotle said, meaning that man is an animal that lives in a *polis*—a city. And both pagans and Christians would agree on putting the family at the base of that society.

But pagans and Christians disagreed quite starkly on what a family should be. And their disagreement was, in the most literal sense, fundamental. It went right back to the roots of what they believed in.

For Christians, God himself is a loving family. The Father loves the Son; the Son is obedient to the Father out of love. The love shared by the Father and the Son is the Holy Spirit.

The pagan gods had families, too. But we certainly don't look for *love* in their relationships. Apollodorus summarized the origin of the gods in the shortest possible account. One almost loses count of all the crimes he is recounting.

> *Sky was the first who ruled over the whole world. And having wedded Earth, he begat first the Hundred-handed, as they are named. . . .*

> *. . . But Sky bound them and cast them into Tartarus, a gloomy place in Hades as far distant from earth as earth is distant from the sky.*

> *And again he begat children by Earth. . . . And again he begat children by Earth, namely, the Titans. . . .*

But Earth, grieved at the destruction of her children, who had been cast into Tartarus, persuaded the Titans to attack their father. . . . And they, all but Ocean, attacked him, and Cronus cut off his father's genitals and threw them into the sea; and from the drops of the flowing blood were born Furies, namely, Alecto, Tisiphone, and Megaera. And, having dethroned their father, they brought up their brethren who had been hurled down to Tartarus, and committed the sovereignty to Cronus.

But he again bound and shut them up in Tartarus, and wedded his sister Rhea; and since both Earth and Sky foretold him that he would be dethroned by his own son, he used to swallow his offspring at birth. . . .

Enraged at this, Rhea repaired to Crete, when she was big with Zeus, and brought him forth in a cave of Dicte. She gave him to the Curetes and to the nymphs Adrastia and Ida, daughters of Melisseus, to nurse.

So these nymphs fed the child on the milk of Amaltheu; and the Curetes in arms guarded the babe in the cave, clashing their spears on their shields in order that Cronus might not hear the child's voice. But Rhea wrapped a stone in swaddling clothes and gave it to Cronus to swallow, as if it were the newborn child.

But when Zeus was full-grown, he took Metis, daughter of Ocean, to help him, and she gave Cronus a drug to swallow, which forced him to disgorge first the stone and then the children whom he had swallowed, and with their aid Zeus waged the war against Cronus and

the Titans. They fought for ten years, and Earth proph-
esied victory to Zeus if he should have as allies those
who had been hurled down to Tartarus. So he slew their
jailer Campe, and loosed their bonds. And . . . the gods
overcame the Titans, shut them up in Tartarus, and
appointed the Hundred-handers their guards; but they
themselves cast lots for the sovereignty, and to Zeus was
allotted the dominion of the sky, to Poseidon the domin-
ion of the sea, and to Pluto the dominion in Hades.[1]

This was how the world of the pagan gods began. Twice a father tries to rid himself of his children; twice a furious wife conspires with her children against their father. The ruling gods are those who succeeded in a war against their own father. It is not that human beings brought sin into the world; on the contrary, the gods themselves set the example of violence, murder, parricide, and betrayal.

Compare this to what the Christians had to say about the origins of the world:

In the beginning was the Word, and the Word was with
God, and the Word was God. He was in the beginning
with God; all things were made through him, and with-
out him was not anything made that was made. In him
was life, and the life was the light of men. The light
shines in the darkness, and the darkness has not over-
come it. (John 1:1–5)

From the beginning, the Father and the Son have been in perfect harmony, because they are the same God. "No one who denies the Son has the Father. He who confesses the Son has the Father also" (1 John 2:23).

In the Trinity, Christians have a model of perfect love. There is no betrayal, no conflict, but only unity. The God the Christians worshipped was a model of perfect love, an example to live up to.

The stories of Cronus and Zeus, on the other hand, gave pagan believers a model to live down to.

A Pornographic Culture

Consider Rome of the late first and second century AD—but don't judge by what you see in museums. Be grateful, instead, that today's curators have some sense of decorum. For the remains of imperial Rome are overwhelmingly pornographic.

Common vases, lamps, and jewelry were festooned with the most shockingly obscene images. And the walls of Pompeii— their lurid details preserved by the ash from Vesuvius—show us that those little household objects were the tip of the iceberg. The decorations in the homes of the middle class were little different from what could be found in the common rooms of the brothels. Often the images were scenes from pagan mythology, the amorous adventures of gods and demigods; they were both pornographic and religious at the same time.

For all the culture's pornographic cast, Roman thinkers recognized that lust got in the way. The Stoics, as we've already mentioned, believed that the best way to subdue lust was to indulge it and get it over with; then a person could go back to his pursuit of detachment. Some pagan cults threw wild orgies; some were served by eunuchs. Sex was everywhere in ancient Rome, but there was really no place for it in Roman philosophy. It was an inconvenience, a need of the body to be indulged when it became pressing but otherwise to be ignored.

But if it was hard to find a place for sex in ancient philosophy, sex was everywhere in Roman culture. Those obscene images we know from Pompeii decorated the walls of ordinary rooms. The children grew up with them.

And was there anything wrong with that? The innocence of children was not a high priority, especially in the families of the very rich. Parents usually left the raising of the children to the hired help, and the hired help were anything but reliable.

In a family with any pretense to status, the children were turned over to the supervision of a loyal slave. In Roman comedy, the "loyal" slave was a stock character, the cunning schemer who put on a great show of loyalty but was only looking out for himself.

Parents who sent small boys to school assumed that the tutors would molest them.[2] The popular entertainments of the day are full of pederasts—some portrayed as dirty old men, but some as quite ordinary people. Much of the convoluted plot of Petronius's *Satyricon,* a rambling picaresque novel of Nero's time, has to do with a love triangle between the hero, his friend, and a little boy. Remember that many, in some places perhaps most, of the girls were killed at birth. There was a decided imbalance in the sexes, and the scarcity was bound to have an effect on sexual behavior.

With limitless leisure time and no supervision, teenaged

boys roamed the streets in gangs. They passed time in mischief, random sexual activity, and, now and then, raping a prostitute. If the prostitute was a girl, she might have been in a brothel because she had been rescued from a dunghill when she was a baby. (Christians and pimps were the only people likely to rescue an abandoned girl, though they did so from very different motivations.) She might be very young, because having invested in feeding and caring for her, the pimp would want to start making a profit as soon as possible.

Meanwhile, the girls who did grow up at home—and by the end of the first century AD they were in short supply—were married off very young. Custom dictated that the girl's father had to pay a substantial, sometimes ruinous, dowry to the groom for taking her off his hands. Girls suffered misery on two fronts: the groom was very often interested more in the money his bride would bring with her than in the bride herself; and the father could think of his daughter only in terms of the fortune she was costing him.

When the wedding did come, the pagan instinct for combining pornography with religion was on full display. The wedding guests celebrated the wedding by singing bawdy songs. It was rather a disappointment if the new bride was willing and didn't have to be forced. "The wedding night," writes the French historian Paul Veyne, "took the form of legal rape."[3]

According to marital custom, the newlywed girl could look forward to a predatory relationship, rife with sodomy, abortion, and contraception. Adultery was expected of men, and, at least in rich families, of women as well. Private detectives prowled the streets of Rome, spying on wives whose husbands suspected that they were raising a son who looked exactly like the milkman.

This was what a Roman marriage was like—and why should it be any different? The marriages of the gods were exactly the same. Juno fumed and plotted revenge while Jupiter left a trail of bastard demigods across the Mediterranean world. We become what we worship. If divinity behaves this way, then humanity will follow.

So marriage could be loveless and miserable, and in a certain sense it was expected that it would be loveless and miserable. But if marriage grew too miserable, divorce was easy. All it took was for one party to leave home with the intention of divorcing.

These standards were reflected in popular entertainment. Tertullian, explaining to Christians why they should avoid the theater, provides a description that is colorful but fairly accurate, to judge by the plays that have survived:

> *Are we not, in like manner, enjoined to put away from us all immodesty? On this ground, again, we are excluded from the theater, which is the very home of immodesty. . . .*
>
> *Even the harlots, victims of the public lust, are brought upon the stage, their misery increased because there they are in the presence of their own sex, from whom alone they usually hide themselves: they are paraded publicly before every age and every rank—their abode, their gains, their praises, are set forth in earshot of those who should not hear such things. . . .*
>
> *If we ought to abominate all that is immodest, on*

what ground is it right to hear what we must not speak?
For all licentiousness of speech, nay, every idle word, is
condemned by God. Why, in the same way, is it right
to look on what it is disgraceful to do? How is it that
the things which defile a man in going out of his mouth,
are not regarded as doing so when they go in at his eyes
and ears? . . . You have the theater forbidden, then, in
the forbidding of immodesty.[4]

Public entertainment in Rome was just like life, but on the stage. And when Romans tired of sex, they flocked to the circus to see criminals tortured and killed by beasts or by gladiators. This was family entertainment; we know from ancient graffiti that boys idolized star gladiators the way boys of today idolize football quarterbacks.

The Attractions of Childlessness

The world where the early Christians raised their families and the early Christian priests exercised their ministry was what might be called a culture of death.

Life ought to have been something like paradise. The world was at peace. Material prosperity had never been greater. Even the ordinary Roman had things that would have been unobtainable luxuries a few generations before.

Caesar Augustus, the emperor at the time that Jesus was born, was praised as a savior by the Roman people. Through military might and diplomacy he unified lands and people stretching from Great Britain to Egypt, from Morocco to Georgia. He suppressed rebellions and practically eradicated piracy, creating the conditions for unprecedented trade and prosperity—especially for Roman citizens. What were once luxuries of the rich became necessities for the middle class. Taxation of the provinces ensured that no one in Rome need ever want for food or entertainment. There would always be bread and circuses.

The people should have been happy. Wasn't this a perfect world in which to raise a family!

But already during Augustus's reign (27 BC–AD 14), the Romans were facing a crisis. With all their wealth, they grew accustomed to an unmoored, leisurely lifestyle, drifting from pleasure to pleasure . . . without the encumbrance of children. There was little incentive to marry. The tendency was to drift from one gluttonous dinner party to another, one wine-inspired hookup to the next.

Augustus noted this problem and foresaw that it would be disastrous for the economy and for homeland security.

He needed his people to reproduce. So he tried to legislate a solution. He outlawed adultery, fornication, and homosexuality and threatened transgressors with flogging or death. He imposed punitive taxes on men and women who remained single. Similar taxes were laid upon married couples who had few or no children. "And yet," lamented the pagan historian Tacitus, "marriages and the rearing of children did not become more frequent, so powerful were the attractions of childlessness."[5] His contemporary Pliny the Younger spoke of the "burden" of having even one child and the "rewards of childlessness."[6] In one of the great ironies of ancient history, all of Augustus's family-oriented laws were enacted during the consulship of two bachelors, Papius and Poppaeus. Both had chosen to remain single and childless in spite of all the penalties![7]

Their flouting of the emperor's policy set the tone for the enforcement of those laws. The laws were a joke, and the emperor himself was hardly a model of the kind of citizen he was trying to encourage. Augustus was married three times before he ascended to the throne, and he had only one child.

In times of prosperity, people looked at the fines and decided that they could afford them. They were lifestyle expenses. Various emperors after Augustus tried to encourage childbearing through legislation, but their efforts uniformly failed. Rome could not require spouses to trust each other. Rome could not require a person to defer gratification of any desire for the sake of another person. Rome could not impose a requirement for citizens to transcend their petty desires for the sake of the common good.

The imperial government in Rome, for all its marvelous achievements—which included clean water, the rule of law, and the suppression of piracy—could not compel its citizens to trust in the future. Lacking that hope, Romans didn't want children, and so they didn't have them. . . . Or at least they didn't raise them up. Instead, they put their effort into the pursuit of pleasure. Clement of Alexandria observed that the same people who killed their newborns nevertheless lavished attention and money on their pets. "They expose children that are born at home, and take up the hatchlings of birds, and prefer irrational to rational creatures."[8] The wealthy who put their children out with the trash sometimes buried their dogs and cats in elaborate tombs.

From Owner to Lover

Often miserable people are people who are looking for answers. Why is the world the way it is? Why don't we live in paradise? What can we do so that we're not so miserable all the time?

As we've already seen, many Roman intellectuals sought answers in Stoicism. But Stoicism could take them only so far. Life stinks, it said, and in a short time you will die. Between now and then, your only hope was to detach your inner self from the world so that you wouldn't feel the pain anymore.

For people looking for answers, that program wasn't ultimately satisfying.

New mystery religions from the mysterious East gained some foothold among the middle classes. Romans studied the arcane wisdom of the Egyptians or the mysteries of Mithra hoping to find answers, especially if those answers gave them license to go on living their comfortable material lives.

At first Christianity must have seemed like yet another of those faddish Eastern religions. But it didn't take long for the Roman establishment to determine that Christianity was something else entirely—and the proof that the Romans put Christianity in a different category was that the authorities quickly banned it, whereas they continued to tolerate other religions.

Christians set themselves apart by refusing to take part in the impure and cruel customs of daily Roman life. We have many sermons and tracts from those years—such as the one we saw from Tertullian—condemning the grossness of the theater, the sickness of the circus, and the licentious bedroom behavior that was prevalent among the pagans. As the *Epistle to*

Diognetus tries to explain to a pagan audience, what makes the Christians different is not that they live different lives, but that they live the same lives as the pagans but in a unique way.

> *They marry, as everyone does; they beget children, but they do not destroy their offspring. They have a common table, but not a common bed. They are in the flesh, but they do not live after the flesh. They pass their days on earth, but they are citizens of heaven. They obey the prescribed laws, and at the same time surpass the laws by their lives. They love all men, and are persecuted by all.*[9]

But what is more remarkable is the testimony of the pagans themselves. The Romans were frankly astonished by the Christians, because the Christians routinely achieved something the Romans had thought impossible: Christians preached and practiced a range of virtues that involved sexual continence—chastity, purity, and even lifelong celibacy. The great pagan physician Galen wrote: "Their contempt of death is patent to us every day, and likewise their restraint in cohabitation. For they include not only men but also women who refrain from cohabiting all their lives; and they also number individuals who, in self-discipline and self-control, have reached a peak not inferior to that of genuine philosophers."[10] Most Stoics, who supposedly despised human passion, believed that sexual passions were best quelled by indulgence.

Celibacy was hard for pagan Romans to understand, but the self-discipline and self-control it required were qualities a Roman could admire. Even married Christians strove for chastity and true love. Theirs was a radically different kind of marriage compared to what Romans were used to. Their devotion and constancy to each other suggested that marriage might be a fountain of happiness, rather than an obligation to be grudgingly endured.

What was this secret the Christians had that seemed to give them happy marriages, and even made them happy when they decided to live celibate lives? It was a mystery—a mystery in the most fundamental sense of the term. For Christians, marriage was not just a business arrangement that allied two families; it was a sacred bond, a sacrament, instituted by God, that made the husband and wife "one flesh."

"One flesh"—what does that mean? Paul gave the church in Ephesus some famous advice about married life:

> *Be subject to one another out of reverence for Christ.*
> *Wives, be subject to your husbands, as to the Lord. For*
> *the husband is the head of the wife as Christ is the head*
> *of the church, his body, and is himself its Savior. As the*
> *church is subject to Christ, so let wives also be subject in*
> *everything to their husbands. Husbands, love your wives,*
> *as Christ loved the church and gave himself up for her,*
> *that he might sanctify her, having cleansed her by the*
> *washing of water with the word, that he might present*
> *the church to himself in splendor, without spot or wrin-*
> *kle or any such thing, that she might be holy and with-*
> *out blemish. Even so husbands should love their wives*
> *as their own bodies. He who loves his wife loves himself.*
> *For no man ever hates his own flesh, but nourishes and*

cherishes it, as Christ does the church, because we are
members of his body. "For this reason a man shall leave
his father and mother and be joined to his wife, and the
two shall become one flesh." This mystery is a profound
one, and I am saying that it refers to Christ and the
church; however, let each one of you love his wife as him-
self, and let the wife see that she respects her husband.
(Ephesians 5:21-33)

This advice seems so commonplace, even old-fashioned, these days that we're likely to miss how revolutionary it was in the ancient world. To a Roman man, a wife was property, just as children were property. A woman had no legal existence apart from the men who controlled her—her father until she was married, her husband afterward, her son if she was a widow and lucky enough to have a son. If no man owned her, she was nobody at all. Children were no better off. Traditionally, a Roman father retained the legal right to execute his children if he judged them guilty of a crime, even into adulthood. They were his children; they belonged to him.

The fundamental family relationship in Rome was the relationship of owner to property. Yet Paul tells husbands to be ready to die for their wives, just as Christ died for the Church. To a good Roman, steeped in Roman family values, this was little better than nonsense. You might love your wife, but die for her? You might love your chariot, but it would make no sense to die for it. If you died, your chariot would be of no use to you.

Paul's advice makes sense only if a wife is a person, not a

piece of property. Romans understood the idea of friends dying for friends, equals dying for equals; that was good and noble. Paul is saying that your wife is your equal in the same way that your friend is, and you should regard her life as *more* precious than your own.

Marriage as a Sacrament

It was Christian morality, and the evident love in Christian families, that gradually converted the Roman Empire. In following Paul's simple but radically different advice, early Christians found the happiness that was eluding pagan Rome at the height of its prosperity. They had left behind the loveless world and revealed a new and better world. Think of the ideal home life of today: a mother and father who love their children and are equal partners in raising them. Imagine how this picture would have shocked a well-bred pagan Roman.

The second-century Greek philosopher Celsus found reprehensible the idea that women would have influence in the education of children.

> *In private houses we see workers in wool and leather, and laundrymen, and the most ignorant hicks, not daring to speak a word in the presence of older and wiser masters. But when they get hold of the children privately, and certain women as ignorant as themselves, they pour out wonderful statements, telling them to pay no attention to their father and to their teachers, but obey them. . . .*

They must leave their father and their teachers, and go with the women and their playmates to the women's apartments, or to the leather shop, or to the laundry, and thus reach perfection. And by words like these they win them over.[11]

The idea that women could have anything to teach these children was as appalling to Celsus as the idea that lower-class tradesmen could have anything to say that was worth hearing.

For a good Roman, the "family" was simply an extension of the father. He spoke, and they obeyed. From the point of view of Roman tradition, the single most revolutionary thing in Christianity was Paul's startling instruction "Husbands, love your wives."

The statement carries more theological weight than we realize, because after all these centuries of Christianity we find it hard to imagine that there was a time when husbands weren't supposed to love their wives. Yet in ancient Rome, a gentleman who obviously loved his wife was sneered at. His wife was his property, not his equal. If she was the best kind of wife, she might act as a sort of head butler, keeping track of the slaves and the more trivial aspects of household management. Mainly, though, she was good for breeding heirs. Yet that role was not associated with a reciprocal, loving relationship. The Roman gentlemen we meet in literature were more likely to reserve "love" for the exalted philosophical friendships between equals that they theoretically prized, although in fact backstabbing was more the rule than friendship among the Roman upper classes. A man could be infatuated with his mistress, or with a pretty young boy, but that was lust—*eros*—the lowest form of love in the philosophical hierarchy.

Exalted love—the love of friendship—had no place in marriage. The ceremony was an acknowledgment that the husband was getting what he wanted. Except for the fun part (and the novelty wore off rapidly), marriage was a business transaction.

In contrast, for the Christians, marriage was a *sacrament*. It is a sign and an image of the love between Christ and the Church (see Ephesians 5:32). It was not a business transaction, and it involved far more than a breeding program. It was a sacred union of two people who became *one flesh*. Even after Constantine legalized Christianity, Christian couples still often celebrated their weddings with the old pagan customs—they were fun, after all, and they were what everyone had grown up with. (More than a few of them have survived to our own time.) Many of these customs were not the sort of thing you wanted your priest to see, like bringing burlesque dancers in to liven up the party, so the priest was often excluded from the wedding celebration.

Saint John Chrysostom tried to persuade his flock that they should understand the difference between pagan marriage and the Christian sacrament. He thought they should be appalled by the way weddings were commonly celebrated.

> The custom of marriages has brought in this plague. Or, rather, not of marriages—certainly not!—but our own foolishness. What are you doing, man? Don't you know where you are? You marry a wife for chastity, and to have children. Then what is the meaning of these

harlots? "So that there may be more gladness," someone
says. Madness is more like it! You're insulting your
bride. You're insulting the women you invited. . . .

Marriage is a sweet ointment. So why do you bring
in the foul stench of the dunghill when you're prepar-
ing your ointment? . . . Is marriage a theater? It is a
mystery—a type of a mighty thing! Even if you have no
reverence for the marriage, have some reverence for the
thing it represents! "This mystery is a profound one,"
Paul says, "and I am saying that it refers to Christ and
the church" [Ephesians 5:32]. It is a type of the Church!
And you bring harlots into it? . . . A great mystery is
being celebrated. Out with the harlots! Out with the
profane!

And how is it a mystery? They come together, and
the two make one . . . making not a lifeless image, or
even the image of anything on earth, but of God him-
self. . . . They come, about to be made one body. See
again a mystery of love![2]

Here is the difference between a pagan wedding and a
Christian one. The pagan wedding is a celebration of the pleasure the husband is about to get out of his bride (who, as we
said earlier, is expected not to like it). The Christian wedding
is a sacrament, a union of two souls, an earthly image that mir-
rors the love of Christ for his Church and the love of the three
persons of the Trinity. Neither spouse is acquiring property;
both are coming together to form an indissoluble union.

Christians viewed sex differently than pagans did. It was

not a simple indulgence of the body, and not *only* a means of breeding children. It was an expression of the sacred bond of husband and wife. That's why the context of sex was marriage. And the children produced by that union were part of that love. Girl or boy, "the child is a sort of bridge, so that the three become one flesh. The child connects each to the other on either side." That's what Chrysostom told his congregation. But what if the couple could have no children? Their love was still sacred, and sex was still a sacred thing. "For when they come together it has this effect: it dissolves and mingles the bodies of both."[13]

This was the Christian difference. Instead of a home where the father ruled and the family obeyed, the Christians looked for a home where love abounded. The husband and wife acted together, because they had become one flesh. The ideal home of today—the marriage and family everyone hopes for—is a *Christian* ideal.

To Speak of the Glory That Is Marriage

Back when the persecutions of Christians were still raging, Tertullian wrote a letter to his wife containing one of the most beautiful descriptions ever written of a Christian marriage. This passage would horrify Celsus, because Tertullian assumes that his wife shares every duty, every joy, and every thought with her husband. But it is the perfect picture of what everyone hopes for from a marriage today.

How can I come up with words to tell the happiness of that marriage which the Church cements, and the sacrifice confirms, and the benediction signs and seals—of which angels carry the news, and which the Father ratifies? (For even on earth children do not rightly and lawfully wed without their fathers' consent.) What a union! Two believers, sharing one hope, one desire, one discipline, one and the same service! Both are brethren, both fellow-servants, no difference of spirit or of flesh; they really are two in one flesh. Where the flesh is one, the spirit is one, too. Together they pray, together prostrate themselves, together perform their fasts; mutually teaching, mutually exhorting, mutually sustaining. Both equal in the Church of God; equal at the banquet of God; equal in troubles, in persecutions, in refreshments. Neither hides anything from the other; neither shuns the other; neither is troublesome to the other. They freely visit the sick and relieve the poor. They give alms with no worry; they attend Mass without trouble; they do their daily duty with nothing standing in the way: there is no secret crossing themselves, no trembling greeting, no mute benediction. Between the two echo psalms and hymns, and they challenge each other which shall sing to their Lord better.

When he sees things like these, Christ rejoices. He sends his own peace to these two. Where two are together, he is with them himself. And where he is, the evil one cannot be.[14]

This is the picture of a Christian marriage. Two equal partners, sharing everything in life, acting as one in all their endeavors. It's an ideal picture, and our earthly marriages will never quite live up to it. We'll always have differences and quarrels; we'll always have bits of our lives that are separate. We'll always be sinners.

But what an ideal it is! "Both are brethren, both fellow-servants, no difference of spirit or of flesh; they really are two in one flesh." This kind of marriage was quite foreign to pagan Rome—and at the same time hypnotically compelling. And as our own world looks more and more like the world of the ancient pagans—as divorce, abandonment, and self-indulgence become the rule rather than the exception—that Christian ideal of marriage is still lurking, waiting to turn the world upside down once more.

CHAPTER 4

A REVOLUTION OF WORK

How Labor Became Holy

By the time the Christian Church was about a hundred years old, pagan writers had begun to take notice of it. Celsus, much of whose especially snobbish attack on the Christians survives because the Christian writer Origen took the trouble to refute it almost line by line, was probably typical of the bunch. Celsus was a Roman gentleman—a man who wouldn't think of working with his own hands. Naturally, the thing that seemed to bother him most about Christians was that they were so *lower-class*. A bunch of weavers and tentmakers and shoemakers setting themselves up as thinkers and teachers! What was the world coming to?

One of Celsus's main arguments against the whole idea of the incarnation was that it grew out of poverty. Surely God could have chosen some distinguished lady to be the mother of his child, not a peasant.

Was therefore the mother of Jesus beautiful? And was God connected with her on account of her beauty?— though he is not adapted to be in love with a corruptible body! Or is it not absurd to suppose that God would be enamored of a woman who was neither fortunate nor of royal extraction—indeed, who was scarcely known to her neighbors, and who was also hated and ejected by the carpenter her husband, so as neither to be saved by her own credulity nor by divine power? These things, therefore, do not at all pertain to the kingdom of God.[1]

If, hypothetically, God had wanted to produce a human son, he would have chosen a proper princess to be the mother. Wouldn't he? Certainly he wouldn't choose the wife of a grubby carpenter who had to work with his rough and calloused hands.

And Jesus's disciples were not the sort of men Celsus would want to invite to an upper-class dinner party:

Jesus having collected as his associates ten or eleven infamous men, consisting of the most wicked publicans and sailors, fled into different places obtaining food with difficulty and in a disgraceful manner.[2]

Publicans and fishermen who had to work for their food! Disgraceful. No, that was not the sort of god a well-bred Roman could believe in. What Celsus wanted from a god was something very much like—well, very much like Celsus: a god who was refined enough to look down on the rabble and dismiss them with a bored yawn and a wave of his hand.

What illustrious deed did Jesus accomplish worthy of a God who beholds men from on high with contempt, and derides terrestrial events, considering them as sport?[3]

Celsus takes it for granted that God must be like him. After all, Celsus himself looks down on the working rabble with contempt. The upper class looks down on the lower; that is the order of nature. If God is divine, he must look down on humanity in the same way. And if the Christians worship a lower-class God, then it comes as no surprise to Celsus that the believers themselves are an appallingly vulgar rabble.

What is said by a few who are considered as Christians, concerning the doctrine of Jesus and the precepts of Christianity, is not designed for the wiser, but for the more unlearned and ignorant part of mankind. For these are their precepts: "Let no one who is erudite accede to us, no one who is wise, no one who is prudent—we think these things are evil. But let anyone who is unlearned, who is stupid, who is an infant in understanding, boldly come to be fore the Christians openly acknowledge that such as these are worthy to be noticed by their God; manifesting by this, that they alone wish and are able to persuade the ignoble, the insensate, slaves, stupid women, and little children and fools.

We may see in the forum infamous characters and jugglers collected together, who dare not show their tricks to intelligent men; but when they perceive a boy, and a crowd of slaves and stupid men, they endeavor to ingratiate themselves with such characters as these.

We also may see in their own houses, woolweavers, shoemakers, laundry-workers, and the most illiterate and rustic men, who dare not say any thing in the presence of more elderly and wiser fathers of families; but when they meet with children apart from their parents, and certain stupid women with them, then they discuss something of a wonderful nature. . . . They further add, that if they wish to be instructed by them, it is requisite that they should leave their parents and preceptors, and go with women and little children, who are their playfellows, to the conclave of women, or to the shoemaker's or fuller's shop, that they may obtain perfection.[4]

Shoemakers, cleaners, weavers—these were the people who called themselves Christians. How could a religion made up of such lowly people be anything but contemptible? And Celsus didn't mention the slaves.

The Institution of Slavery

In the ancient world, the taking of slaves was normally the result of conquest. When Rome conquered the Mediterranean world, huge numbers of enemy soldiers and often ordinary citizens on the losing sides became slaves. The children of slaves were also slaves, so in time the slave population grew to be enormous. In some rural districts, almost everyone who worked on the giant factory farms was a slave. No one knows how many people in the empire were slaves, but in Italy, where many of the slaves were sent after Rome's numerous victories, slaves probably composed at least a third of the population.

Slaves had few rights, but they did have some hope. Slaves

could have their own money (though it technically belonged to their masters), and even their own businesses, and they were often free to come and go when they were not working. (Saint Clement of Rome may have still been a slave when he was bishop of Rome.) Eventually, a frugal slave could hope to save up enough to buy the one thing every slave dreamed of owning: himself. A slave who had bought his freedom could rise in society, to a point, and the children of freedmen were free citizens— though as children of slaves they had a mark against them.

That is as much as can be said in favor of the lot of the slave. For the most part, the life of a slave was miserable. Legally, a slave was property a thing, not a person. A slave owner could beat or torture his slave for any reason or for no reason at all. If he decided the slave deserved to die, no one would stop him from killing the slave. People might think he was a fool to destroy valuable property, but they would not think he had committed a crime. He could rape any of his slaves without consequences, and the slave had no right to complain; a well-to-do gentleman might buy a certain number of attractive slaves for that purpose. Under a particularly bizarre twist of the law, the testimony of a slave was not valid in a court of law unless the slave had been tortured first. The slaves who worked on the giant factory farms often died from ill treatment; it was cheaper for the owners to buy new slaves than to provide decent living conditions for their slaves.

When a Roman gentleman like Celsus looked at a slave, he saw a thing, not a person. Slaves were valuable if they served their purpose well; if not, their owner could be rid of them in any number of ways. Cato the Elder, for example, simply threw his slaves away when they were old or sick, turning them out of the house to wander and beg. Slaves who made nuisances of themselves could be sent away to fight other slaves in the gladiatorial schools, or to fight the wild beasts in the arena. (Spoiler: the beasts won.) Slave owners didn't worry about what slaves *thought,* but only about how well they worked.

How could someone like Celsus feel anything but contempt for people who insisted that "there is neither Jew nor Greek, there is neither slave nor free, there is neither male nor female; for you are all one in Christ Jesus"? (Galatians 3:28)

The Indignity of Labor

Celsus was not an especially mean-spirited man. He believed what every Roman gentleman believed: that it was base and ignoble to do useful work with your hands. Aristotle, the most practical of classical philosophers, had explained the matter quite clearly in his *Politics.* Just as the soul rules the body and is superior to it, so men rule beasts and are superior to them, and so the superior men rule the inferior classes of humanity.

> *Domestic animals are superior in nature to wild ones, and for all domestic animals subjection to man is advantageous, as their safety is thereby secured. Also a comparison of males and females shows that the former are naturally stronger and dominant, the latter naturally weaker and subject. And the same law of subordination must hold good in respect of human beings generally.*

Hence wherever there are two classes of persons, and the one are as far inferior to the other as the body to the soul or a beast to a man—and this is the condition of all whose function is mere physical service and who are incapable of anything better—these persons are natural slaves and for them as truly as for the body or for beasts a life of slavish subjection is advantageous. For the natural slave is one who is qualified to be and therefore in fact is the property of another, or who is only so far a rational being as to understand reason without himself possessing it. And herein the slave is different from other animals, as they neither understand reason nor obey it but obey their instincts only. As for the uses to which they are put there is little distinction; for slaves and domestic animals alike render us physical help towards acquiring the necessaries of life.

Now in accordance with these facts it is Nature's purpose to differentiate the bodies as well as the souls of slaves and free persons, making the former sturdy for the satisfaction of our necessary wants, and the latter upright and suited not to employments of this kind but to political life in both its departments, civil and military.[5]

Nature, the rational pagan believed, had intended that one class should rule, and the other vastly larger class should be ruled. The rulers should be men who were suited for ruling: intelligent, educated, and not sullied by mere physical service. The ruled—all the shoemakers and launderers and carpenters and women whose existence was necessary to the perpetuation of the rulers, but who had no time or talent for deep thought—should just shut up and do what they were told. This was what the Roman gentleman believed; Christianity was instinctively distasteful to him because its teachings contravened the established social distinctions. Tradesmen teaching theology! Slaves serving as bishops! What would Aristotle say about such a breach in the natural order of things?

But the problem was that the Roman gentleman himself no longer fitted into Aristotle's neat scheme. And in the back of his mind, he knew it.

Leisure as a Virtue

In the days of the Roman Republic, just before the time of Christ, it was possible for a Roman gentleman to imagine that he was doing something useful. He determined the policy of the state; he meant something to the world, and there would be a hole in the world when he was gone. He didn't have to work for a living, but his leisure made it possible for him to be part of the ruling class of wise and educated men who piloted the state through calm and storm.

The problem was that all the wise and educated men completely bungled the business. The Roman Republic was chronically unstable; even its magnificent conquests were often the product of civil wars rather than deliberate policy. When Augustus restored peace by depriving the Senate and the public officials of all but the show of authority, and became the founder of the Roman Empire, everyone sighed in relief.

But now that the emperor held full power, what was the leisure class for? The whole *cursus honorum*—the career of one public office after another that was supposed to be a gentleman's destiny—was meaningless. Stripped of their real authority, the political offices existed only to be filled by members of the leisure class, and the leisure class existed only to fill the meaningless offices. There was still prestige in being a senator or a consul, but all the ultimate decisions were made by one man—the emperor. The Senate would just nod in assent, and the official just had to check the boxes; there was no thinking to be done.

The upper crust of Roman society filled its days with pleasures. There was, after all, no real business to take care of. Dinner parties went on for hours and sometimes days. There was drinking and debauchery in every form. There were luxuries to be had from far-off half-mythical places like India and China. There were adulterous affairs to dally with and friends to betray—anything to fill the time and make life seem a little less meaningless.

The one thing a proper Roman gentleman would never think of doing to fill his time was productive work. Freed slaves often became fabulously wealthy in Rome—wealthier than the most decadent Roman aristocrat—precisely because they worked at building industrial empires or merchant kingdoms, endeavors that were beneath contempt for established gentlemen precisely because business required *work*.

In the Same Business as God

In contrast, Christians thought work was a good thing.

> *For you yourselves know how you ought to imitate us;*
> *we were not idle when we were with you, we did not eat*
> *any one's bread without paying, but with toil and labor*
> *we worked night and day, that we might not burden any*
> *of you. It was not because we have not that right, but to*
> *give you in our conduct an example to imitate. (2 Thes-*
> *salonians 3:7-9)*

Celsus painted all Christians with the same brush, yet not all Christians were slaves and tradesmen. Even by Celsus's time, there were rich Christians, too, some from the very best families.

But Celsus was right in the main: Christians *did* listen to shoemakers, tentmakers (like Paul), women, and slaves. Those socially inferior beings were treated as if they were just as important as anybody else.

Archbishop José H. Gomez[6] points out that the Christians derived a radically different view of work from reading the Hebrew Scriptures. In the Old Testament, work is depicted as a necessity of the human condition, and as honorable. Even in paradise, there was work: Adam was placed in the Garden of Eden "to till it and keep it" (Genesis 2:15)—and that was before the Fall. To the Israelites, there was nothing undignified in the ancestor of all humanity having been a gardener—or their greatest king, David, having been a shepherd. God himself labored to create the world, and then he rested. The Israelites followed the same pattern in observing a Sabbath day of rest each week.

The idea of working for six days and taking the seventh day off was very strange to Romans, who thought the Jews must be a lazy nation. (Ironically, the Romans had so many religious holidays sprinkled throughout the year that they ended up taking off a great many days. But the idea of a *regular* rest from work had not occurred to them.) The Jewish Sabbath—which the Christians transferred to the Lord's Day, Sunday—was something unique in the ancient world.

But why did the Jews take one day in seven off? Not because it was a nice thing to do for the laborers, although it was, but because God had taken the seventh day off, and he had asked Israel to do the same.

> *Remember the sabbath day, to keep it holy. Six days you shall labor, and do all your work; but the seventh day is a sabbath to the Lord your God; in it you shall not do any work, you, or your son, or your daughter, your manservant, or your maidservant, or your cattle, or the sojourner who is within your gates; for in six days the Lord made heaven and earth, the sea, and all that is in them, and rested the seventh day; therefore the Lord blessed the sabbath day and hallowed it. (Exodus 20:8-11)*

We are meant to rest on the seventh day because God rested from creation on the seventh day. He blessed that day and made it holy, and no one can force even the humblest laborer—even a slave—to do work on that day. That's the law.

In effect, the Sabbath exists because your work and God's work are related. You, the humble ditchdigger, are in the same business as God, the mighty creator of rivers and seas. You work in the same way that God works—the God who made man with his hands, as a potter shapes a pot. Instead of something degrading, your labor—no matter how grubby it may be—is something divine. You are a partner with God in creation. After all, God himself was not too proud to get his hands dirty. And your partnership is sealed by the Sabbath, when you rest in the same way that God rested.

Saint Paul, the founder of so many churches and the apostle to the Gentiles, boasted that "with toil and labor we worked night and day" (2 Thessalonians 3:8). He was only following the example of God.

Work and Rest in Proportion

From the beginning, Christians (like the Jews before them) celebrated the work of their hands. They saw work as human participation in the act of creation. We've already seen this idea in Saint Paul, and it comes up again and again in his writing: "We labor, working with our own hands" (1 Corinthians 4:12); "Work with your hands, as we charged you" (1 Thessalonians 4:11); "For we hear that some of you are living in idleness, mere busybodies, not doing any work. Now such persons we command and exhort in the Lord Jesus Christ to do their work in quietness and to earn their own living" (2 Thessalonians 3:11–12). If you're not working, Paul says, you're not acting like a Christian.

The Fathers of the Church picked up that idea from the example set by Saint Paul. The *Didache,* in the first century, exhorts: "If a prophet desires to abide with you, and if he is a tradesman, let him work and eat. . . . See to it that as a Christian he will not live with you idle."[7]

This work ethic was an inversion of pagan values, according to which work was a badge of shame and idleness a virtue.[8]

The Christian was not ashamed to admit that he earned his living. When the Lord's Day came around, the Christian would take the time to rest. This was the pattern God himself set for us: work and leisure in proportion. The pagan thought work was for the servile classes and leisure was for the upper crust. The Christian thought that both work and leisure were necessary for everyone.

The *Didascalia Apostolorum,* a text originating in the 200s, recommends that Christians work diligently when they were not at worship: "All you believers, therefore, whenever you are not in the church, be constant at your labors; and in all the course of your life either be constant in exhortation, or labor at your work and never be idle, because the Lord has said, 'Go to the ant, O sluggard; consider her ways, and be wise' " (Proverbs 6:6).[9]

The reason people should work is not just to produce something useful. Work is something we do for and with God. Some of the freed slaves in Rome worked and got rich (much to the disgust of their former masters), but the Christian had different reasons for working. Work was good for the soul, and it was good for the world.

In the fourth century, the *Apostolic Constitutions* decreed:

"Attend to your employment with all appropriate seriousness, so that you will always have sufficient funds to support both yourselves and those who are needy. In that way, you will not burden the Church of God."[10]

Christ came to give rest to those who labored and found life burdensome. But that didn't mean he came to relieve man from the drudgery of work. He was a carpenter himself, and the son of a carpenter, Saint Joseph, who was venerated by the Church. Jesus took away the burden of work by giving it back its innate dignity.

Because of the value of work, Christians saw the laborer as honorable—as someone who deserved consideration as a person, not just recognition for what he could produce. A Christian might be as contemplative as a pagan philosopher, but he could never forget that God himself was active, forming man with his own hands. He could never forget that active work was something divine. God had worked for us, and we should expect to work for God and for others.

We have proof that the early Christians saw dignity in their work. Some of the grave markers in the catacombs and ancient cemeteries bear the symbols of trades that Christian men and women had practiced in life. They were marks of honor: having a trade meant that this man or woman had not burdened the Church, but indeed had enriched it. By the works of their hands, they had cooperated with God in the task of the ongoing creation and redemption of the world (see Colossians 1:24).

As Christianity moved from the underground to the mainstream, these Christian ideas about the dignity of labor and the humanity of the laborer began to percolate through the Roman

world and eventually bubbled up into the law. The idea of setting aside one day out of seven as a day of rest was finally made
law in 321. Constantine, the first Christian emperor, created the
weekend by a decree:

> *On the venerable Day of the Sun let the magistrates
> and people residing in cities rest, and let all workshops
> be closed. In the country, however, persons engaged in
> agriculture may freely and lawfully continue their pur-
> suits; because it often happens that another day is not
> so suitable for grain-sowing or for vine-planting; lest
> by neglecting the proper moment for such operations the
> bounty of heaven should be lost. (Given the 7th day of
> March, Crispus and Constantine being consuls each of
> them for the second time.)*[11]

We notice that the law is carefully worded to be neutral as
far as religion is concerned. It mentions nothing about worship, and it applies to pagans, Christians, and Jews equally.
An exemption is made for agricultural work (in addition to
Constantine's stated reasons, it is likely that pagans still pre-
dominated in the countryside). Constantine calls the day by its
pagan Roman name—*Dies Solis*, or Day of the Sun—rather than
"the Lord's Day," as the Christians called it. In keeping with
his policy of religious tolerance (see Chapter 8), Constantine
imposed no rules about what people were supposed to do with
their day off.

There is no doubt that the Jewish idea of the Sabbath, now
spread by the Christians, was behind this legislation. And,

simple as it is, this new law shows a vital change in how the law treated ordinary people. Tradesmen are not seen as beasts bred for shameful toil, as Plato and Aristotle imagined. They are not simply means of production. They are persons, with a right to a life of their own beyond the workshop. Constantine brought the full force of imperial law down on the side of Christian egalitarianism. The laborer was as much a person as the emperor, and his work was no less important or holy.

Work, Wealth, and Charity

Something happened with the Christian revolution that couldn't be undone. By the late 300s, for the first time in history, we find a philosopher (Saint Gregory of Nyssa) arguing on religious principles for the abolition of slavery. Many centuries would pass before his arguments had any widespread practical effect, but never again would it be possible for serious thinkers to say that a common laborer was really nothing more than a beast. That doesn't mean we have always treated our laborers well— but even when we don't, we feel obliged to pretend that we do. A Roman aristocrat could argue that his slaves were just beasts of burden; a modern executive doesn't have that luxury.

The change in the perception of work was most obvious in the way the best of the Christian leaders approached the problems of labor and management.

Saint Basil the Great (330–379) was a bishop, theologian, and reformer. As bishop, he established a modus vivendi for the Church in its dealings with secular authorities. As an ascetic, he composed a set of rules that continue to govern monasteries today. As an administrator, he founded institutional charities that established a model for the Church's future philanthropic work.

He guided his metropolitan church through a great social crisis in 368, when a series of natural calamities—including hailstorms, floods, and earthquakes—brought famine to the region of Cappadocia. Basil was appalled when some merchants seized the opportunity to grow rich from the scarcity of food, leaving the poor to starve. Basil shamed the wealthy through his preaching and induced them to share what they had. He led by example as well; he sold his inheritance and gave the proceeds over to relief efforts.

If we want to pick one writer among the Church Fathers whose work is the foundation of the Church's social teaching, Basil would be the man. Concern for the poor and the duty of working to alleviate their misery are recurring themes in his homilies and letters, most of them addressed to groups of ascetics. The ideal monk, Basil wrote, was one whose prayer was augmented by work, but whose work was done so "that they may have something to distribute to those in need."[12]

Fortunately, Basil's position as bishop of Caesarea gave him the power to put his ideas into action. All his thought came together in brick and stone in a huge establishment known as the Basileidas. It was a vast complex of facilities built to serve a variety of needs—so vast that the locals referred to it as "the New City," as if it counterbalanced the city of Caesarea. Gregory of Nazianzus compared it to the Seven Wonders of the Ancient World. There was a soup kitchen to feed the hungry.

There were poorhouses to shelter the homeless. Significantly, there was a trade school that helped beggars find a way out of poverty and dependence. A hostel gave shelter to needy travelers and kept them out of the notoriously immoral wayside inns. The elderly and the dying were cared for in nursing homes.

These facilities were staffed by an army of male and female ascetics who gave food and medical care to everyone who approached, regardless of their religious affiliation. This work was not something they did in addition to their devotions; it was integral to their religious life. This mixed life of prayer and action was Basil's ideal.

But the duty to serve the poor applied to all Christians. In appealing to the rich, Basil often emphasized that it was in their own best interest to succor the poor, since they would be judged worthy of heaven based on the charity they demonstrated on earth. In Basil's world, charity thrived on industry— the industry of both the monks and the businessmen—and the industrious became the beneficiaries of those they assisted.

In his eulogy for Basil, Gregory of Nazianzus described Basil's life of work and charity as "the short road to salvation, the easiest ascent to heaven."[13] Furthermore, it was a life recommended for all Christians. Imagine how Celsus would have sneered at such an idea—that working with your hands to feed the poor should be the short road to salvation! Basil's theological reflection produced insights that would be key to the development of a distinctive Christian social ethic. When one of his correspondents seemed a little too much in awe of Basil's position as bishop, Basil wrote back to tell him that no one was really above anyone else. All human beings were equal by nature, Basil said.

> You have done well to write to me. You have shown how great is the fruit of charity. Continue to do so. Do not think that when you write to me you need offer excuses. I recognize my own position and I know that by nature every man is of equal honor with all the rest. Whatever excellence there is in me is not of family, nor of superfluous wealth, nor of physical condition; it comes only of superiority in the fear of God.[14]

Nor could one tribe or nation claim superiority over another:

> The saints do not all belong to one country. Each is venerated in a different place. So what does that imply? Should we call them city-less, or citizens of the whole world? Just as at a common meal those things laid before the group by each are regarded as available to all who meet together, so among the saints, the homeland of each is common to all, and they give to each other everywhere whatever they have to hand.”[15]

Basil lived in the Roman world of industry, giant commercial enterprises, international travel, and shady politics—but he lived his life completely by the principles taught by Christ. For him, we were all one in Christ, and the poorest laborer was the equal of a bishop. A Christian could entertain the idea that a laborer was superior to someone who lived idly. For Christians, labor was a way of reaching toward the divine, not a distraction from the life of the spirit.

Pray and Work

Already by Basil's time, men who wanted to devote their lives to something transcendent were withdrawing to monasteries. As a series of disasters swept over the empire, ultimately shrinking and fragmenting it beyond recognition, the monasteries became the intellectual centers of European life, the places where a promising young man would be sent to be educated. In many ways monasteries were the successors of the philosophical schools of teachers like Aristotle.

But there was one enormous difference. Monks were not men of leisure. True, they made time to pray all throughout the day, but even the best-educated among them also had to dig ditches, plant crops, grind flour, or copy manuscripts. There were no class distinctions among the monks, no men who were set apart for a life of leisure on the grounds that they were presumed to be superior to the laboring herd. The proof that a monk was striving after holiness, that he was developing as far as it was possible for a human being to develop, was that he was working hard.

It was in the monasteries that the new Christian ideas about work really came into their own. Some of the monasteries became holy factories, where the monks turned out goods that could support the community. In the early 300s, Saint

Pachomius organized his monasteries in Egypt according to trades. He had smiths, gardeners, tailors, carpenters, dyers, tanners, shoemakers, copyists, and camel drivers on the roster. Altogether there were at least three hundred monks toiling away in his monastery, making their work a prayer.

And though the monks had withdrawn from the world, their labor was for the benefit of the world. The Benedictines, for example, were the public works department wherever government was no longer able to take care of the infrastructure. They put the roads back together; they shored up falling bridges. They cultivated their fields to grow food for the poor.

The revolution in the world's attitude to work can be summed up in Benedict's motto, the one by which Benedictines still live today: *Ora et labora*—Pray and work. In the Christian, as in Christ, those activities are distinct yet united.

CHAPTER 5

A REVOLUTION OF RELIGION

God Is Love

W hen Peter confessed his faith in Jesus as "the Christ, the Son of the living God," Jesus responded by praising him for understanding what was being revealed to him. Then Jesus went on to say, "and on this rock I will build my *church*" (Matthew 16:13–19). At this point, the disciples must have smiled, nodded, and thought to themselves, *Riiiiiight . . . wait . . . what's a church?*

We use the word *church* as if it's the most natural concept in the world, but in the ancient world it was something entirely new, something that Jesus created. To be fair, the word was not new. The Greek word *ekklesia* meant "a gathering of an assembly of people," originally the calling to arms of a military regiment.[1] But it is precisely the revolutionary nature of the word *church* (rather than the word *synagogue*, which would have been the expected term) that demonstrates that Jesus was consciously making a break with what had come before him; he was starting something completely new.[2] Jesus gathered his disciples, taught them about the kingdom of God, and gave them the authority to baptize, to re-present his incarnation and passion at the eucharistic table, and even to absolve sins, and in doing all of this, he founded something the likes of which the world had never seen before—he founded the Church.[3]

This Church that Jesus founded with his apostles was a revolution of religion in three important ways. First, Christianity redefined the way that humans relate to the Divine. The relationship between Greeks and Romans and their gods was a relationship of patronage, in which the people hoped to please their gods enough to receive protection and blessings. The Hebrew people, the nation of Israel, were in a covenant relationship with their God, and they were expected to remain faithful to God in order to avoid the consequences of infidelity, and to live a life of blessing. But Christians enter into a relationship with God as *individuals* responding to an offer of forgiveness, which is, at its heart, God taking the initiative to reach out to people in mercy and compassion. Those individuals who respond to God's invitation are then gathered into a community of mutual care and support, and they reflect the grace they had received from God toward one another. In the Christian faith, God is not only the transcendent Creator and Judge; he is also relational—up close and personal, and intimately involved in the lives of people and their relationships. God cares about people. God is love (1 John 4:7–21).

Second, Christianity redefined the way that humans understand God. For the Greeks and Romans, there were many gods, and even demigods or other beings who were quasi-divine. For the Hebrews, there was one God, but direct contact with him was rare and reserved for a select few. For Christians, the one God can be known in Jesus Christ and is present in the Holy Spirit. With the coming of Jesus, something unprecedented had happened. He was "God with us" (Isaiah 7:14; Matthew 1:23). The Divine had become human (John 1:14), and the Son of God had come to reveal the Father (John 1:18). The revelation of God (and of who God is) was more direct. Because God is love, God had reached out to humanity by extending himself into the created world and the human realm.

But the incarnation created a new problem. While humanity's blessing (playing host to the Divinity in the person of Jesus Christ) made a more direct and intimate understanding of God possible, it also begged the question of how God could be understood as *one* if in fact the Son of God is also divine. In other words, how could Christians remain faithful to their Hebrew monotheistic roots and at the same time claim that it was appropriate to worship Jesus Christ? How could God be one and also be incarnate in Jesus? The answer is that God is a Trinity, that Divinity became personal to us by becoming one of us.

Third, the understanding of God as a Trinity of three divine persons means not only that God is in relationship with humanity, but also that God is *internally* relational, that Divine love is constantly shared among the Father, Son, and Holy Spirit, and that this loving relationship has existed since long before humans entered the picture. The relational nature of God, along with the extension of God's love into the human realm, led the Christians to conclude that the very nature of the Church required that it must also be an extension of God's love in the world; in other words, it must be inclusive. Unlike other ancient religions that were specific to a particular ethnic or geographical group, or open to only a certain segment of society, the Church was open to all: Jew or Greek, slave or free, male or female (Galatians 3:28; Colossians 3:11). To put it another way, because God is love, God is a Trinity, and because God is a Trinity, God is therefore relational and invitational. God reaches out to all people, inviting them into a community of reconciliation—the Church. The Church gave to the world a gift—or rather, God gave the world a gift through the Church. It is a revolution of revelation, so to speak. The revelation is that God is love, which means that God is relational and compassionate, and that God's love is offered to all people.

In these three ways, Christianity reshaped how the world would relate to the Divine in worship and prayer.

God Is Love

Before Christianity, religion was a service contract. For the most part, ancient religion entailed people serving various gods (usually by ritual sacrifice) so that the gods would protect people or grant them blessings—in effect, doing whatever it was believed would coax or motivate the gods to do *the people's* will. For most ancient religions, doing the will of a particular god was not an issue. First, the will of the gods could hardly be known, apart from oracles and soothsaying. To make things more difficult, the multiple gods could be at odds, and sometimes a person had to play a guessing game to decide which side they should be on. Trying to influence the outcome of a war became more a matter of praying to the more powerful god than putting together the more powerful army.

The Hebrews did not have to guess which god they should serve. Their God (who was the only God) had taken the initiative to reach out to them, and to tell them what he expected of them. In the Old Testament, the relationship between the Creator and a nation of people is marked by a covenant. The Jews promised to do God's will, rather than their own will. Even when the people failed to keep their side of the agreement, God proved unfailingly faithful to the covenant. And even when the people's unfaithfulness caused a separation from God, God showed mercy and offered reconciliation. Thus the foundation for the revolution of religion was laid.

Some of the pagan philosophers recognized one god—or as they saw it, a high god over all the other gods—who had a will that should be obeyed. But in the early forms of what we would call "qualified monotheism," the reason for doing the high god's will was to secure blessings in the present life.[4] Socrates believed that people would have better lives if they tried to live within his high god's will, but he was not saying that his god was personally involved in people's lives, only that it was in everyone's best interest not to fight against the natural laws instituted by this high god.

What made Christianity revolutionary was that it was more than a service contract; it was a relationship with the Divine. What is more, this relationship was not limited to a particular nation of people; it was a relationship in which God made himself personally available to all individuals. Equally significant, the relationship with God extended beyond the present life into an eternal afterlife. Put another way, Jesus himself and the apostles after him were working with a new definition of the concept of *salvation*—one that assumed a person's eternal destiny depended on a response to God's self-revelation in Jesus Christ. And that self-revelation was the very embodiment of God's love. Once and for all, God had reached out to humanity in love, offering reconciliation and relationship with the Divine, and he did this in a particular time and place, in the person of Jesus Christ.

For the most part, salvation in the ancient world was understood in the context of divine protection. People prayed to be rescued from whatever danger was present at the moment. Salvation had little or nothing to do with an afterlife. Many, if not most, ancient people believed in an afterlife, though the majority believed that life after death was little more than a shadowy continuation of the present life. A few of the mystery cults promised a happier afterlife for their devotees, and some ancient peoples hoped to be reunited with their ancestors after death. Jewish apocalyptic writings hinted that God's salvation might extend beyond this life, but what Jesus said about the kingdom of God went beyond this and was entirely new. He combined the Hebrew concept of the "Day of the Lord" with a new emphasis on salvation as eternal life, presenting the human-divine relationship as one that was for the here and now and also for eternity.[5]

The urgency with which the early bishops and theologians debated their understanding of Christ and the Trinity was owing to their belief that a wrong understanding risked salvation itself. To believe the wrong thing about Christ, was to believe in the wrong christ, and the wrong christ was not one who could save. Thus the Church's greatest hope was not just to make it through this life in as good a state as possible, but to be the bride reunited with her Groom in the eternal Kingdom of the Father.

The Greco-Roman philosophers did have a concept of an immortal soul and an afterlife. But they taught that the soul's goal was to be free of the body, to discard it in favor of a disembodied existence. Some, like Plato, taught that the soul would be reincarnated into many successive bodies before it finally sloughed off the flesh forever and ascended to a purely incorporeal existence. The Church rejected these ideas, teaching instead that the human body is part of God's good creation and is therefore an essential part of what it means to be human. Christians taught, not freedom from the body, nor reincarnation into successive bodies, but the resurrection of the body. In the middle of the second century, the Christian philosopher Justin Martyr wrote a document on the doctrine of resurrection, in which he said the following:

> *And there are some who maintain that even Jesus himself appeared only as spiritual, and not in the flesh. . . . these people seek to rob the flesh of the promise. . . .*

> *. . . In the resurrection the flesh shall rise whole. For if on earth he healed the sickness of the flesh and made the body whole, much more will he do this in the resurrection, so that the flesh shall rise perfect and whole. . . .*

> *But in truth, he has called even the flesh to the resurrection, and promises to it everlasting life. For where he*

promises to save humanity, there he gives the promise to
the flesh. . . . And God has called the human person to
life and resurrection, he has called not a part, but the
whole, which is the soul and the body. . . .

. . . Why did he rise in the flesh in which he suffered,
unless to show the resurrection of the flesh?[6]

As Justin and others described it, the human body is an essential part of the human person, not a shell to be discarded but a product of God's good creation. In the end, it is the whole human person who receives salvation, not the "spiritual" part only. Christian salvation is not a disembodied cosmic union with the Divine that results in the absorption of the individual into God and the individual's loss of self. God cares for the whole person, whom he created in his image, and whom he loves enough to want to save for an eternal relationship.

Christianity took religion to a new level in another way. The purpose of worship was not to appease the supernatural powers who might grant people an easier time in their daily lives. It was not a contract between God and a particular group of people who hoped for divine protection from the dangers of the world, or who resigned themselves to live within the natural laws for the sake of a peaceful existence. The Christian religion offered a different kind of hope: a salvation defined as reconciliation with God—reconciliation that results in union with God, and ultimately resurrection of the whole person. In other words, the Christian religion acknowledges God's offer of love. God invites every individual into relationship with himself, a relationship that embraces the whole person—body, soul, and personality—and a relationship that never ends, because God's love never ends.

God Is a Trinity

Greco-Roman religion was primarily an attempt to explain the universe by projecting human qualities (including the worst human characteristics) on a cast of cosmic characters who could be credited with (or blamed for) the existence of whatever seemed hard to explain. For pagan worshippers, the needs and desires of multiple gods (who often had conflicts with one another, betrayed one another, and acted out of lust, pride, and anger) explained why things were the way they were in the world. Creation was often explained as the result of cosmic procreation, in which a male deity impregnated a female deity and thereby created life.

Polytheism, the belief in multiple gods, was based on the assumption that different gods must be responsible for different spheres of life. There was a god of love and a god of war, a god of agricultural production (fertility, harvest) and a god of agricultural barrenness (winter). There were gods for serious matters and gods for partying. A multitude of gods shared responsibility for even the most mundane events—anything that was outside the control of human beings in the ancient world. There were gods who watched over the city, and gods who watched over the household; there were gods who guided the stars, and gods who guarded the hearth.[7]

The more philosophically minded among the Greeks and Romans were at times a bit embarrassed about the stories of gods behaving badly, so they interpreted the myths as allegories. Some of these thinkers began to move in the direction of monotheism. But as we have noted, theirs was a qualified monotheism, with a high god who ruled over the other gods, and even their high god, though he might have been benevolent, was impersonal and uninvolved in the lives of believers. In addition, the high god of the philosophers was not offended by people's continued worship of the lower deities. This is one reason that it would be inaccurate to say that the philosophical high god was the same as the truly monotheistic God of the Hebrews and Christians. The one God of the Jews and the Christians did not allow people to worship other gods, let alone angels or other "principalities and powers" (Colossians 2:18).

The people of Abraham's clan gave up believing in multiple gods (or at least they were supposed to) because the one God had revealed himself to Abraham. Among their many names for this one God was El Shaddai, which can be translated as "God the all sufficient One," that is, the God who needs no other. This one God does not need a counterpart to create life. This one God does not share the responsibility for the universe with any other gods. And this one God does not share his authority with other gods who have different spheres of influence. The people of Abraham, Isaac, and Jacob were supposed to listen to their God as he revealed himself to them, rather than presume to conceive of gods made in their own image. They had been given the gift of the revelation that there was only one God, who was ALL-mighty and ALL-knowing.

Thus monotheism was a revolution in itself. Christianity built on the foundation of Hebrew monotheism and became a revolution of the revolution, with the advent of Jesus Christ and the Church he founded. The teachings of Jesus and the apostles redefined (or perhaps further clarified) monotheism.[8] But how could the Christians claim to be faithful to the monotheism of their Hebrew roots and also claim that Jesus Christ was the incarnation of Divinity? How could Christ be divine and God still be one? The question was answered gradually, and over time, as the apologists, bishops, and theologians of the Church worked through the implications of the two natures of Christ: his full humanity and his full divinity.

The doctrine of the Trinity is already evident in the earliest documents of the New Testament (see 2 Corinthians 13:14; Romans 8:9; Matthew 28:19). In fact, the seeds of the doctrine of the Trinity are planted in the Old Testament.[9] For example, in the book of Isaiah, God is referred to as "Father" (Isaiah 63:16; 64:8), and we also read of God's Holy Spirit (Isaiah 40:13; 61:1; 63:10–11, 14; see also Psalm 51:11–13). In addition, there are several places in the Old Testament where the early Christians discerned an appearance of the pre-incarnate Christ (for example, Genesis 18), not to mention the many prophecies of the Old Testament that were fulfilled by the coming of Jesus.

Furthermore, from the earliest writings of the Church Fathers, such as the episcopal letters of Ignatius of Antioch, the apologists' open letters to the emperors, and the treatises of early theologians such as Irenaeus of Lyons, it is clear that Christians understood that Christ has two natures, and to deny this was *heresy*. There were those who said he was human but not divine; and there were others who said he was divine but not human. From the very beginning, the mainstream Church rejected an either-or approach and affirmed both of Christ's natures.[10] Jesus Christ is fully human, as we are (but without having given in to temptation); and he is also fully divine, as the Father is, (yet the Father and the Son are not one and the same). This latter point begged the next question: If Jesus Christ is divine but not the same as the Father, then what is his relationship to the Father, and how can it be understood in a way that does not imply that there are two Gods? The answer to the question is the doctrine of the Trinity.

Although the building blocks for the doctrine of the Trinity (that is, the revelation that God is triune) are given in the pages of Scripture, it took some time for the theologians of the early Church to put those building blocks together and clarify the doctrine. The teachings of Jesus were preserved and passed on by his apostles, who taught their own disciples how to interpret Scripture in light of the person and message of Christ. Those disciples of the apostles effectively became the first bishops—the first leaders of local Christian communities. Thus the teachings of Jesus and the authoritative interpretations of the apostles were handed down to the next generation and the next by the early bishops, who were the successors to the apostles. This process is often referred to as *apostolic succession*. Eventually, the bishops met in councils to ratify and clarify the Church's teachings, and to preserve the unity of the Church—that is, to make sure all the local churches were on the same page, so to speak. One result of this process was the historic definition of the faith known as the Nicene Creed.

The doctrines of the Church are the natural and logical result of this process of apostolic succession, in which the Church's authoritative interpretations were handed down through the generations by an unbroken chain of bishops, going all the way back to the apostles, and through them, to Jesus himself.[11]

The Church's theology of the person of Christ and his relationship to the Father reached a zenith in the fourth century, in response to a controversy over an Alexandrian priest named Arius. He was teaching a version of that heresy which denied the full divinity of Christ, and he was gaining followers. The debates over this question led to the convening of the first *ecumenical,* or worldwide, council of the Church: the Council of Nicaea in the year 325. But the council did not completely end the controversy, and the ongoing debate (along with the persistence of the heretics) led to the second worldwide council, the Council of Constantinople in 381. From these two councils in the cities of Nicaea and Constantinople emerged the statement of faith known as the Nicene Creed. This creed clarified the Church's understanding of God as Trinity, and with it, the Church eventually converted the empire and the world to this understanding. As the creed explains, God is a Trinity, and that includes Jesus Christ, who is *consubstantial,* that is, of the same divine essence, as God the Father.[12] In other words, the Father and the Son are *one divinity;* they are one, but not one and the same; they are distinct but not separate. The one God reveals himself to humanity in three manifestations, or "persons," known to us as the Father, the Son (Jesus Christ), and the Holy Spirit.[13] And the second person of the Trinity, Jesus Christ, is the embodiment of God's love for humanity.

The concept of monotheism, and in fact the concept of divinity itself, was clarified based not on human speculation but on God's self-revelation in Jesus Christ. And the Christian Church clarified these concepts in ways that were unprecedented, and these concepts would influence how the majority of the world's people would understand God.

On the one hand, Christian theologians argued that because God is omnipresent and omnipotent, there must be only one God, since omnipresence and omnipotence leave no room for the influence of other gods. The theologian Tertullian criticized the belief in many gods as illogical. He argued that since the Romans believed there were too many gods to know them all, they must necessarily offend the gods they did not worship. Around the turn of the third century (200), he wrote:

> *You worship, some one god, and some another, of course you give offense to those you do not worship. You cannot continue to give preference to one without slighting another, for selection implies rejection. You despise, therefore, those whom you thus reject; for in your rejection of them, it is plain you have no dread of giving them offense.*[14]

In other words, he was saying, if you're not afraid of offending those gods you do not worship, then those gods have no power, and that means they do not really exist. Therefore, Tertullian argued, belief in multiple gods is not rational, and in fact the omnipotence, omnipresence, and omniscience of the one true God rule out the existence of other gods.

On the other hand, the Christian God is not so transcendent as to be impersonal, as the philosophers believed their "high god" was. The Christian God is directly involved in the world in ways that go beyond simply sustaining creation. God is *personal,* which means that God is relational; he seeks relationships with people. Not with nations only, but with individuals too. Yes, God is transcendent (above and beyond created space and time), but God is also immanent (up close and personal). The incarnation is proof of God's desire to be in relationship with humanity. Furthermore, Jesus and his apostles told us that through his Holy Spirit, God lives within us (John 16:13–15; 1 Corinthians 6:19).

Although it seems to be a paradox, God as Trinity is a perfect balance of transcendence and immanence. As transcendent, God is omnipotent Creator; as immanent, God is compassionate Reconciler, extending his invitation of love to all. God is also a perfect balance of harmony in unity, three in one, and it is the love shared by the three persons of the Trinity that is offered to humanity. This is what Christians have always believed, and this is what they have taught the world. Thus the doctrine of the Trinity stands out as one of the most significant contributions that the Church has given the world: one God in three persons—one of whom was Jesus Christ: one person in two natures, divine and human. In other words, the incarnation is the ultimate expression of God's love, in which he reaches out to humanity in revelation and invitation, in the divine persons of the Son and the Holy Spirit. Therefore, God is a Trinity precisely *because* God is love.

As it turned out, the Arian controversy led to an ongoing

debate over the two natures of Christ, and it became clear through the ecumenical councils of the fifth century that the union of divine and human in the person of Jesus was the lynchpin of humanity's union with God. Because Christ is fully divine, he is united with the Father and the Holy Spirit in the one Trinity. But because Christ is also fully human, he is united with humanity through the bond of a common human nature. Thus our hope for union with God depends on the union of the two natures in the person of Christ. We humans can know God because our humanity is united with God in the person of Christ. Therefore, our salvation depends, not only on what the Savior did, but also on who the Savior is. God's love is extended into humanity through the human nature of Jesus Christ, and humanity is reconciled to God through its union with his divine nature.

Finally, Saint Augustine, writing on the Trinity around the turn of the fifth century, made the connection between the love of God and the internal relationships among the three persons of the Trinity. He wrote that because God is a Trinity, God is eternally in relationship, and that relationship is always a relationship of love. The concept that God is love is inseparable from the concept that God is a Trinity, since it is the love shared by the Father, Son, and Holy Spirit that is also shared with humanity and extended to individuals. In fact, it is God's love that defines what love is for humanity. As such, the Church taught the world that the love of God is not only invitational; it is extravagantly inclusive, offered to all people as an extension of God's compassion.

The Church Is Inclusive

Christianity was born into a world where religion was, by and large, an enterprise of self-preservation. The traditional Greco-Roman mythologies required sacrifices to a god or gods who were thought to protect the city or nation, mostly out of fear that the failure to appease the gods would result in catastrophe. Participating in the imperial cult was primarily a matter of civic duty, an expression of patriotism and loyalty to the emperor, but again it was motivated by the fear that the failure to do so would bring unwanted results. But regardless of whether a person truly believed in the gods or participated in the rituals only out of obligation, the religions of the Roman Empire were social —not in the sense that people had a responsibility to one another, but in the sense that people had a responsibility to their city, empire, and emperor. What a person really believed and what a person did behind closed doors were immaterial as long as that person fulfilled his or her patriotic duty by participating in the cults that promoted the government.

On the other hand, some of the mystery cults of the Roman world advocated a kind of personal devotion, but they did not include expectations that the believers would care for one another, let alone care for those outside the group. To the extent that religion was practiced by the individual, it was an application of the Roman patron-client system on a grand scale. The human client served the divine patron in exchange for favors that the patron could grant. Thus some ancient religions had components of individual belief, and other religions had aspects of social or cultural expectations, but none of them (with the exception of Judaism) combined the social aspects of a community of faith with individual responsibility for both devotion to God and compassion for others.[15] Behavioral expectations were a matter of law, not of religion, and in general most religions did not require members to be concerned for the well-being of others, even those devoted to the same gods.

Christianity, building on the foundation of Judaism, is not social only or individual only. It is about more than fulfilling a civic duty or attempting to gain a better life for oneself. It is a balance of personal belief and social responsibility. What is more, it is devotionally exclusive, requiring that belief in the one God means rejection of all other gods. The Church was evangelistic, rejecting a facile "live and let live" detachment in favor of a conviction that this new understanding of God, and how to have a relationship with God, was good news that needed to be shared. The God of love expected his devotees to have personal faith and to be concerned for their individual salvation, but he also expected them to share the love—to be focused outside of themselves, to be other-centered, and to take responsibility for the welfare (even the salvation) of others.

As the Church debated, explained, and clarified this new understanding of God and salvation, the early Christians were in a very real sense defining the Church and Christianity itself. If the disciples had indeed asked, *What's a church?*, that question took a while to answer. But as it was answered, the followers of Jesus were creating a new world—one in which the expectations of what it meant to be a responsible (and respectable) person and citizen were being revised according to the revealed will of the one God.

So how would the Church define itself? First of all, Christianity is a religion of conversion, meaning that one becomes a Christian by making a decision. It is not a religion of "race," which means that being born into a particular ethnic culture is not a prerequisite for membership. The Christians distinguished themselves from their non-Christian neighbors by the Church's rite of initiation: baptism. Baptism included, and still includes, an identification with Christ: in going under the water we identify with his death, and in rising up from the water we identify with his resurrection. Christian baptism entailed making a commitment to the faith, but it also meant renouncing all other faiths and rejecting the worship of all other (supposed) gods. It entailed promising to try to live up to the behavioral expectations of the Church (as we will see in more detail in the next chapter).

Of course, today many people are Christian because they were born to Christian parents, but in the early centuries before the legalization of Christianity, this was not necessarily the case. Especially in the period of time covered by the New Testament, there were very few second-generation Christians, and this is why most baptisms in the New Testament are assumed to be adult baptisms. For these people, membership in the Church required a choice. This was the reason the Western Church eventually (by the third century) separated confirmation from baptism, to give those baptized as infants the opportunity to confirm their baptism by their own choice.

The believer was meant to choose to join the Church through the exercise of free will, a God-given capacity that is part of what it means to be made in the image of God.[16] Since religious truth is revealed by God to humans, and this revelation comes in the form of an invitation that demands a response, Tertullian wrote, "[People] are made, not born, Christian."[17]

There were some Roman cults with initiation rites, and some of these even resembled a kind of baptism (probably in imitation of Christian baptism), but these cults were neither monotheistic nor devotionally exclusive. People could join multiple cults, but they were always expected to continue to participate in the civic religion involving the traditional mythology. On the other hand, some cults were exclusive in the sense that they allowed only women or only men to join. Many of the mystery cults, such as the one devoted to Mithras, were more like fraternities than houses of worship. The initiations often cost new members a lot of money, and their rites included ancient forms of hazing (devotees of Mithras made male pledges dress as women and wait outside in an anteroom while the already initiated members enjoyed their dinner). These events included all the elements of a fraternity party, including heavy drinking and sometimes even the use of hallucinogenic drugs. Yet in spite of this social aspect of the cults, there is no evidence that they carried any expectation of concern for fellow members outside of the rituals.

By contrast, the inclusive nature of the Christian Church flowed from Christian convictions about God. The God of the Christians was not the object of a "mystery cult" in which the devotees were left to their own devices to create gods in their own image. The one God is a God who reveals himself to humanity, and that revelation reached its height at the incarnation of Jesus Christ. The beliefs of his followers are based on their own experiences with him—in person with the apostles, and continuing in the Church with the presence of the Holy Spirit. And what the Christians learned about God from Jesus and the apostles was that God was eternally loving, mercifully compassionate, and inclusively invitational. Thus the Christians naturally concluded that the Church and its members must be all of these things as well.

In the third and fourth centuries, two controversies arose concerning the Church's theology of baptism and the sacraments. In the third century, some who had denied the faith to save their lives during times of persecution wanted to return to the Church. Others who had converted to Christianity through a separatist sect, or who had possibly been baptized by someone who had denied the faith, also wanted to come into the Church. Bishop Cyprian of Carthage and some others believed that these people should not be reconciled without being rebaptized. Pope Saint Stephen I of Rome opposed them, arguing that the baptism of these people was still valid, even if they had been baptized by someone whose faith had lapsed.[18] In the early fourth century, after the Great Persecution, the debate came up again, this time with regard to ordination.[19] Known as the Donatist controversy, the debate centered on this question: If a bishop was consecrated, or a priest was ordained, by someone whose faith had lapsed, was that consecration or ordination invalid? And if so, would that mean that all the sacraments presided over by the bishop or priest in question were also invalid?

The conclusions the Church reached on these issues were another step in the Church's self-definition, because these questions got to the heart of how Christians understand the Church. Led by Pope Saint Stephen of Rome and Saint Augustine of Hippo, the Church concluded that the effectiveness of the sacraments is not dependent on the faith of the presider, or even on the faith of the witnesses.

Pagan Roman religion, on the other hand, featured soothsayers reading omens. The presence of an unbeliever (i.e., a Christian) among the assembled was thought to render the soothsayer unable to correctly read the omens. But Christian ritual is not rendered impotent so easily. It is not fragile because God makes the sacraments effective, not the human presider. The one God is not fickle or capricious; he is faithful and keeps his promises. Therefore it is God who baptizes, God who confirms, God who ordains, and ultimately God who sends the Holy Spirit to dwell within and empower believers. Any lack of faith, or even mortal sin, on the part of the priest or bishop cannot thwart the work of God.

The Church affirmed that what was important about a baptism was not whether the presider was without sin (for who could ever hope for this, let alone know it?), but rather whether the baptism rite was an initiation into the one true God or some other (false) god. Specifically, this means that as long as a person is baptized in the name of the Trinity—the Father, Son, and Holy Spirit—the baptism is valid. When this principle is applied to ordination and the validity of the sacraments in general, it means that we can trust the sacraments of the Church, regardless of what is going on in the heart of the one presiding.

The concept that a sacrament is effective simply because it is correctly conducted (*ex opere operato*) by a properly ordained representative of the Church is relevant today, especially in light of the unfortunate reality of clergy abuse. God is faithful, even when Church leaders are not.

The practical application for this concept was clearly demonstrated during the controversies of the third and fourth centuries. Those who advocated for rebaptism often appointed themselves as judges of which clergy were worthy to preside, and even whether certain individuals could be reconciled to the Church or should be excommunicated.

To be excommunicated from the Church was to be excluded from the table of communion. So in one sense the Church defined itself as those who gather around the eucharistic table. It is no coincidence that the Church is described as the *Body of Christ* (1 Corinthians 12). In the early days of the Church, there were no buildings designated as "churches." The Church was collectively the members of the Body of Christ, and the congregation of the Church in any given city was simply the people who gathered around the eucharistic table to receive his Body and Blood. It was through the sacrament of the Eucharist that one participated in Christ, remained in Christ, and anticipated the heavenly banquet that he described (Matthew 22:1–14). If teachers gathered followers on the basis of alternative interpretations that were at odds with the Creed, and if those teachers were confronted with their error and refused to change their teachings and accept the Creed, they were officially excommunicated. In other words, they were considered (at least temporarily) outside of the membership of the Church, even though they had been baptized. Therefore, just as the Church could be defined by membership according to baptism, the Church could also be defined by table fellowship according to the sacrament of the Eucharist. In a very real sense, the Church *is* the table.

The Donatists and others like them presumed to try to purify the Church by excommunicating, or excluding, those whom they considered impure, but Church leaders such as Pope Saint Stephen and Saint Augustine knew that the Church must not try to weed the fields prematurely (Matthew 13). The Church should not seek to purify itself by excluding anyone. Certainly Jesus's ministry was not one of exclusion, but of inclusion. Following his lead, the Church is meant to include everyone, so that as many as possible might be saved. This is the original meaning of the word *catholic* (lowercase *c,* meaning, "universal") when applied to the Church—not only that the Church exists worldwide in every geographical location, but also that the Church exists for all people. The Church cannot be for some only; it must be open to all, regardless of sex (unlike some of the mystery cults), social class, ethnicity, or language (Galatians 3:28). Thus the Church even rejected one of the Romans' most cherished cultural proclivities—marking off social class distinctions—by blessing illegal mixed marriages of different social classes.

As the Church continued to define itself, it did so in ways that made it unique among organizations in the ancient world. Everyone was invited, and once inside, all were valued equally.[20] The Church rejected distinctions of ethnicity, economic class, and even distinctions based on perceptions of who was more or less righteous. The Church was not meant to be a country club for those who had "arrived"; it was a school for those on a journey. It was not an enclave for the perfected; it was a hospital for the sick of soul—a hospital in which everyone admitted that they were afflicted with the disease of sin and were in need of the medicine of the sacraments.

The Church further defined itself by teaching Christians what it meant to remain in the Church and be true to their relationship with the Trinity. Some of the martyrs gave their lives for their faith as catechumens, before they were able to be baptized or receive communion (it was believed that their martyrdom was their baptism—a baptism in their own blood). Baptism was no guarantee of salvation. Being baptized cleansed one from original sin, and washed away any sins a person might have committed before baptism, but the early Christians did not believe that baptism washed away future sins or guaranteed perseverance in the faith. The many Christians who denied the faith to save their lives during times of persecution were evidence of this. Baptism gave a Christian a clean slate but not a free ride. It was necessary to *remain* in Christ (John 15:1–7). And since Christ is found and met in the sacraments, and the sacraments exist only within the Church, remaining in Christ means remaining in the Church.[21]

Remaining in the Church means remaining in the *true* Church, not joining a fringe or separatist movement led by a teacher of heresy. In other words, the Church was also defined by its doctrine, because it was the doctrine (and specifically the doctrine of the Trinity) that defined what Christianity was. To be Christian was to accept the doctrine of the Trinity. Therefore to reject the mainstream (orthodox) understanding of God as

Trinity and Christ as both divine and human was to be outside the Church. One literally excommunicated oneself by rejecting the conclusions of the ecumenical councils and the consensus of the bishops, who were the successors to the apostles.

The Arian controversy had demonstrated that the unity of the Church depended on unity of belief, at least insofar as the major doctrines were concerned. The bishops of the Church could not afford a "live and let live" attitude toward doctrine because to deviate from what the Church was teaching was to deviate from what Jesus and the apostles had handed down. Souls were at stake. To believe in the *wrong* christ (for example, one who was not fully divine) could not lead to salvation, and so the heretics were not simply people who had an opinion of their own; they were teachers who were leading innocent believers astray, and possibly to their damnation. The Church could not simply let people believe whatever they wanted to believe. The Church had to be clear about what it taught, because to teach something that was not consistent with the teachings of the apostles, the Church fathers, and the councils of bishops, was to be something other than the Church.

Therefore, the unity of the Church was based on a common understanding of God as Trinity as well as participation in the sacraments. The Church was inclusive with regard to people, but it was doctrinally and devotionally exclusive, demanding unity based on a commitment to the one triune God alone. Those who gathered at the table, regardless of where they were in the world, were one in Christ. They were united with one another, and with God through Christ. This union was the Church—it was not something created by mere humans, but ultimately it was created by God and founded by the Son of God and his apostles. And this is what Jesus promised could not be destroyed, or even discredited—for the gates of hell could not prevail against it (Matthew 16:18).

Conclusions and Consequences

Most of the other religious options in the Greco-Roman world tended to be exclusive with regard to membership—either only certain people were allowed or only a particular ethnic group was included—but these cults were inclusive in that people could worship whatever gods they chose. Christianity was the opposite. It was exclusive to the one God—and by choosing to become Christian, one was choosing to reject all other gods— yet it was inclusive in welcoming all people. The Church was a radical departure from Roman tradition and culture; it was countercultural, and therefore it was often seen as antisocial. Although Christians were persecuted, the Church did not turn against the world, but rather converted it. And it did so by clarifying what the Church was and what Christians believed about God in ways that were rooted in God's ancient revelations of himself, but also newly interpreted through the apostles' experience with Jesus.

First, the incarnation demonstrated that God is not only the transcendent Creator; he is also immanent and wants to be in relationship with individuals and involved in their lives and in human history. Therefore, God has revealed to humanity a certain amount of understanding about the divine nature, an understanding that achieved a new clarity with the coming of Jesus and the writings of his apostles. We know that we are created in the image of God, and we do not presume to create God in our own image, with all of our human weaknesses, needs, and desires. We know that God has a will for us, and we are expected to do God's will, not try to get God to do our will. We know that God keeps his promises, and that he remains faithful, even when we fail in this regard. Our relationship with God is not fragile because God is patient and merciful. What is more, since God is our Creator and is not burdened by the kinds of weaknesses that characterize sinful humanity, God can do something to help us. God is concerned for our well-being because we are his creatures, made in his image. God is both *interested* in us and *compassionate* toward us. Put simply, the idea that *God is love* is a revolution of religion.

Equally important, we know that God is a Trinity: Father, Son, and Holy Spirit; and that Jesus Christ is the divine Son of God and the central figure of human history—worthy to be the object of our faith. Though it is a mystery that cannot be fully understood, we know that God is the perfect balance of harmony in unity. This is important, since the Trinity can be seen as the model for the Church and for other human relationships. In other words, what we believe about God informs what we believe we should be as God's people. The Church balances diversity within its unity. It is inclusive, accepting all people, but not to the point of accepting all opinions or interpretations—for that would threaten its unity. Still, if God is patient and merciful, this means that we are also supposed to be patient and merciful toward others. Since there are none who do not fall, the Church reconciles those who admit their failings. Thus membership in good standing is based on humility, not perfection.

There are Christian denominations today (many of those that would be called fundamentalist) that are operating with the mind-set of the Donatists of the fourth century. They feel the need to protect their congregations from the impure and exclude those whom they think are unworthy. Some even presume to rebaptize those who come to them from other denominations.[22] But the early Church came to the conclusion that impurity is not the danger; pride is the danger, because pride leads to the breakdown of unity. The Church concluded that the worst sin a person could commit was to divide the Church. Therefore, the unity of the Church was preserved through inclusion. The *catholic* (i.e., universal) Church was to be inclusive, extending the invitation of relationship with God in Christ to everyone, regardless of ethnicity, social class, or sex. All people are invited to membership in the Church, and then once initiated in baptism, they are invited to the table of the Eucharist.

It is also important to remember that the Church rejected any kind of dualism that proposed a division of spirit and matter, especially if it implied that the material world is less valuable—or worse, disposable. Often today when we see a lack of respect for creation, it comes from exactly this kind of dualism that the early Church rejected. But equally dangerous is the dualism that presents the human body as something to be discarded in the afterlife, implying that it can be denigrated in the present life.

Following Jesus's lead, the Church revolutionized how the world would understand salvation and the afterlife. The hope of humanity is not what the philosophers taught: enduring reincarnation until one finally transcends the material world to become a disembodied spirit. Rather the hope of humanity is the resurrection of the whole human person—including the body, which is good because it is created by God. Jesus had combined the concepts of afterlife, salvation, and resurrection into what he called the kingdom of God. It is worth noting that this means we get only one chance at life, so it's important to live with purpose and reverence (see Hebrews 9:27). Most important, however, is the realization that our salvation depends not only on what the Savior said and did but also on who the Savior is. Because he is not human only but also the incarnation of full divinity, it is wrong to say that he is just a good example to follow, or that "the message matters more than the man." These are exactly the kinds of the things the early heretics like Arius would have said, and unfortunately we still hear them today.

In a world where religion was either social without being personal, or personal without being social, Christianity embraced both personal belief and social responsibility. It was a religion of free will, entered into by individuals out of faith, but a faith that also included expectations that members would care for one another and work together to care for others in the name of Christ. Christian worship was not (and should not be) motivated by a desire to coax divine favor, but rather by gratitude for the compassion God shows to humanity. The Church defined itself in opposition to the other religions of its day, drawing boundaries in terms of initiation (baptism), doctrine (that God is a Trinity, as outlined in the Creed), and the table of the Eucharist (the anticipation of eternal life, which Jesus described as a heavenly banquet). It was within those boundaries that one would experience the radical concept that God is love.

A REVOLUTION OF COMMUNITY

Love Your Neighbor

When the ancient philosophers spoke of ethics, it was more about how to behave as a good citizen so that society would not become barbaric, rather than about following the moral code of a higher authority. In other words, while ancient cultures had their behavioral codes, these codes were a matter of law, not religion per se. If we are to accept the writings of Plato as representative, philosophical ethics were a matter of self-preservation: *Don't do unto others whatever you don't want them to do unto you.*[1]

For Socrates, even with his belief in a god who had a will, there was really no such thing as sin. Wrongdoing sprang from misinformation. People only did the wrong thing because they thought they were doing the right thing, but they were simply misinformed about what was the right thing to do in that particular situation. Socrates and Plato taught that if people only knew what was right, they would do it. There may be a kernel of truth in this, but it does not adequately take into account the realities of human nature—the fact that most people will often do what feels right for themselves in the moment, even when they know it may hurt others.

In general, Roman religion allowed people to assume an attitude of "religious, but not spiritual"—that is, people fulfilled their duty to society by continuing the traditional worship of the old mythologies, but they did not feel obligated to order their lives based on their beliefs (if they had any). Or to put it another way, ancient people showed that they were good citizens by remaining observant of cultural and social norms and traditions, but they reserved the right to do whatever they wanted as long as their behavior did not bring shame on themselves, their family, or their cult. Ironically, the end result is similar to what we see today among those who say that they are "spiritual, but not religious." They feel entitled to believe whatever they want to about the spiritual realm, without imposing any restrictions on their behavior.

In our world, the word *religion* implies standards for behavior in everyday life. In the Greco-Roman world, it did not. Having said that, it is true today that even many self-proclaimed Christians do not feel obligated to live by the moral code of their religion. This is just more evidence that our world is becoming increasingly like the world in which the early Christians were persecuted—and what is worse, many people within the Church are playing for the other side.

In contrast to the gods of the Greco-Roman religion, the God of the Hebrews required his people to care for the widow, the orphan, and even the stranger in their midst. The prophets proclaimed that it is a sin for the powerful to oppress the weak. And when Jesus came along, he pressed these expectations even further. He raised the bar on morality, expanding the precept that we care for others to include those outside our own group. It is well known that Jesus changed the "eye for an eye" rule, asking us instead to turn the other cheek. He even made the willingness to forgive others a factor in our salvation (Matthew 6:14–15, 18:23–35).

Following Jesus's lead, the Church has always insisted that we respond to the love of God by loving our neighbor. And the answer to the question "Who is our neighbor?" (Luke 10:29–37) could no longer be limited to those who are like us. The Church expected its followers to share the love of God with everyone— even those outside the boundaries of the community—thus redefining the concept of *community* as something that really has no boundaries.

A major portion of early Christian catechesis (in which new converts prepared for baptism) was education in morality. Believers had to know how to live as a Christian in the world before they could be baptized, and adapting to this radical difference in behavior formed an important part of the Christian identity. Christians distinguished themselves from their pagan neighbors by the difference in their lifestyle. Morality was one of the markers of a Christian, but the moral expectations were not limited to how Christians treated other Christians. The expectations were extended to include the *ministry* of Christians to all people.

When we talk about Christian morality, we are not talking about a morality based simply on a kind of natural law, for if that were enough, then Plato would be right, and it would be enough to be a good pagan. Truth—moral truth—is not discovered by humanity; it is revealed to humanity by God, and that revelation has come to the world through the Christian Church.

In our culture there is no excuse for not knowing God's will because the Church has given society the gift of communicating God's will to the world. This is the good news of what the Catholic Church calls the New Evangelization: that God has reached out to us. We don't have to try to coax God to do what we want him to do, because God already loves us and wants to bless us—but that also means that God communicates to us his expectations. And the beauty of Christian morality, as we will see, is that it is contagious—in a good way—spreading the antidote to the toxins of pagan culture.

Doing God's Work in the World

In a previous chapter, we touched on the concept of free will; all humans have been given the gift of free will by virtue of the fact that we are created in the image of God. This means that, though God loves us, he gives us the choice as to whether we will accept a relationship with him, and he expects that if we choose to do so, our decision will be motivated (at least in part) by love for God—love returned for love. The gift of our free will, and the blessing of a relationship with our Creator, also means that we have a responsibility to respond to other human beings in a way that is consistent with our relationship with God. Free will comes with the responsibility to be accountable for our choices and actions, and the responsibility to care about other people, who are also made in God's image.

In the early fifth century, Saint Augustine found himself at the center of another controversy, one that brought the theological implications of Christian morality into focus. A monk named Pelagius challenged Augustine's belief that a person can only do God's will if God first empowers him to do it. The ensuing debate resulted in the writing of many more documents (an ongoing "debate on paper") and several councils. The whole affair came to be known as the Pelagian controversy, and it took about a hundred years for the Church to sort out the issues.

On the surface, the controversy seemed to be over the concept of free will. But on a deeper level the issue was anthropology—how the Church understood the human person and the human potential for good. Saint Augustine was skeptical of people's ability to resist temptation and avoid sin, so he argued that anything good that comes from humanity—from good deeds to personal salvation—is the result of the work of God's grace in a person's life. Therefore, Augustine developed a strong doctrine of original sin, and he came to believe that without the enabling power of grace, the human will was not free to do anything positive. As for salvation, each person's eternal destiny was simply a matter of God's choice (or "election"), a choice made before the person was ever born, and without regard to merit or behavior.

Pelagius was more optimistic about free will and human potential. He rejected Augustine's arguments, reasoning that if Augustine was right, a person could avoid responsibility for his actions simply by saying that God had not given him the power to resist temptation. Pelagius believed that Augustine's teachings could be twisted so that God would be held responsible for sin. Pelagius went so far as to reject the doctrine of original sin entirely.[2] In the course of the debate, Augustine and Pelagius pushed each other to opposite extremes, with Augustine arguing that the human will is completely fallen (totally depraved) and any good work is the result of the power of grace alone, and Pelagius arguing that a person can do good works (even resulting in salvation) by free will alone. Pelagius said that because perfection is possible, God therefore expects it of everyone.

The argument came down to the question of who is behind the good works that result from a Christian's relationship with God. Is it all the work of God (Augustine), or is it all the work of the individual exercising free will (Pelagius)? The Church eventually concluded that neither extreme was correct, but that the good we do in the world, and in fact even our own salvation, is the result of a cooperation between the human will and God's grace. The Church clarified that God's grace always takes the initiative, so that the human will cannot do good without the prompting of grace, but also that the human will is free to choose good or evil. And while God expects us to choose the good, he does not choose for us. In other words, God invites, coaxes, and empowers, but the individual chooses whether or how to respond.

Thus the Church came to another affirmation of a "both-and" rather than an "either-or" approach. The Church rejected a solution to the question of anthropology that leaned so heavily on grace that it exempted people from responsibility, and it rejected a solution that so heavily emphasized free will and works that it made grace unnecessary. Christianity affirmed the reality of original sin, without making it the excuse for a person's failures, and it affirmed human free will, without being overly optimistic about the potential for human good.

By taking this middle way, the Church affirmed that while original sin is real, we are not totally depraved. We really do have free will, and thus there is an expectation of morality and moral accountability. Still, salvation does not require perfection, since grace includes forgiveness.

As a result of the Pelagian controversy, the Church gave the world the concept of human beings cooperating with God to do the work of God in the world. But equally important is the affirmation that morality and ethics are not simply about understanding what behavior will benefit *us* most in the end; rather morality is other-centered. God invites us to partner with him to extend his love to others. The good news is that overcoming evil is not all up to us, but neither is it all left up to God. Divine Providence moves in the world, and we as Christians are called to use our free will to cooperate with God's grace. In order to realize our creation —and creativity—as creatures made in the image of God, we are to imitate God by embodying God's love toward others. Therefore, if the revolution of religion is that *God is love,* the revolution of the community is that God calls us to *love our neighbor.*

Care for the Poor

The Romans had a tradition of philanthropy, but although the word *philanthropy* means "love for humanity," it's not an accurate label for what was practiced in the ancient world. Like Roman religion, Roman philanthropy was self-serving. The wealthy did not give to the poor; they gave to the city in order to increase their approval rating with the public. They paid for buildings (often pagan temples, but also court buildings and shopping malls) as well as public works. They paid for theaters and amphitheaters, as well as sponsored games and shows, and occasionally they handed out bread or coins to the people who gathered for their spectacles. But they did all these works not out of love for the people, or compassion for the needy; they did it in order to make a spectacle of themselves, to draw attention to themselves and make the people of the city feel indebted to them.[3]

When gifts were given out to the citizens of a city, they were given out according to social standing, so that those who were more needy actually got less, and the destitute were excluded altogether.[4] In the Roman world, and in the ancient world in general, it was assumed that poverty was the fault of the poor, or that it was their "fate." The wealthy had the luxury of believing that everyone got what they were supposed to get, and this justified their habit of ignoring the needy. A few emperors tried to institute a mechanism for feeding the hungry (called the *dole*), but this policy was motivated by a desire to keep the peace—to keep the poor from rioting or from becoming a visible embarrassment in Rome—and it was applied inconsistently and halfheartedly. The government responded only to dire emergencies.[5] Eventually, the Christians stepped in to do what the government could not.

Roman philanthropy meant giving in order to benefit oneself—either to increase one's standing in the community, or to increase indebtedness in those who might one day do something for the benefactor in return. It was widely assumed that if a person could never do anything for you, there was no reason to give anything to that person. Christian charity, on the other hand, means giving without expecting anything in return, and this idea was new in the Roman world.[6] In fact, the word *charity* comes from a Latin word for love, and this label fits, because Christian charity is motivated by love. Charity is a means of sharing God's love on the horizontal plane—by love of neighbor—out of love and gratitude to the God who first loved us (1 John 4:7–21).

As we have noted, Hebrew law commanded that the people of God must have regard for the helpless in their midst. The Christian Church took this principle to a world that blamed poverty on the poor. Even some of Jesus's fellow Jews believed that God rewarded righteousness with prosperity, and therefore poverty must be the result of sin. Much of the Old Testament (not least the book of Job) is meant to argue against this belief. And when Jesus came along, he pointedly posed the question, "Who sinned, this man or his parents, that he should be born blind?" Jesus's answer was: Neither (John 9:1–3). The man's blindness was not the result of sin, but it was an opportunity for the work of God to be done in the world, as a sign of the love of God for humanity. Jesus consistently challenged the assumption that one deserved one's "station in life." Therefore, far from being able to justify ignoring the poor, those with more have a responsibility to give to those with less (see, for example, Luke 16:19–31, the parable of the Rich Man and Lazarus).

Some Hebrew literature went to the other extreme and assumed that it was righteous to be poor and sinful to be rich. And there were some in the early Church who wanted to follow this trend. They took Jesus's words in Matthew 19:24, "It is easier for a camel to pass through the eye of a needle than for one who is rich to enter the kingdom of God" (see also Mark 10:25; Luke 18:25) to the extreme—believing that a wealthy person could not ever hope to receive salvation. But Jesus went on to say, "For human beings it is impossible, but not for God" (Mark 10:27). The second-century Christian teacher Clement of Alexandria wrote a treatise called *Who Is the Rich Man that Shall be Saved?* in order to explain that neither poverty nor wealth are sinful (or righteous) in and of themselves. What matters is how one responds to one's situation—and in particular, he pointed out that the rich person can be saved if he gives to the poor.

Clement's treatise, along with other early Christian documents such as *The Shepherd,* proposed a symbiotic relationship between the rich and the poor. God gave surplus resources to the wealthy specifically so that they would give to those who were in need. It was then the responsibility of the poor to pray for their benefactors that their wealth would not become a spiritual hindrance.[7] The message to the rich was, if you have resources, they are a gift from God—everything you have is a gift from God—and those gifts are meant to be shared.[8] Poverty is not something to be blamed on the poor (so that one can justify ignoring them); the poor provide the rich an opportunity to partner with God—doing God's work in the world by extending God's love and compassion to others. It is a chance to be on God's side, by being on the side of the poor (see Matthew 25:31–46).

Jesus discouraged his followers from thinking of wealth and value as something earthbound. Instead, he wanted them

to understand that true value is spiritual—it goes beyond possessions and it cannot be owned—but it can be shared. He said,
"Do not store up for yourselves treasures on earth, where moth
and decay destroy, and thieves break in and steal. But store up
treasures in heaven. . . . For where your treasure is, there also
will your heart be" (Matthew 6:19–21, NAB). So for Christians,
the storehouses of heaven are the stomachs of the hungry.

From as early as we can tell in the life of the Church, almsgiving has always been considered a form of penance that is an
important part of how we "work out [our] salvation with fear
and trembling" (Philippians 2:12; see also Tobit 4:10 and Sir-
ach 3:29–30).[9] Almsgiving is so important that it is described
in some early Christian documents as being more important
than fasting, or even prayer.[10] For example, the second-century
document known as *The Shepherd* says this about almsgiving:
"Therefore the one who serves God in this manner will live. So
keep this commandment, as I have told you, in order that your
repentance and that of your family may prove to be sincere and
pure and innocent and unstained."[11] Another early document,
known as Second Clement, says, "Fasting is better than prayer,
while charitable giving is better than both, and love covers a
multitude of sins" (cf. 1 Peter 4:8; and Tobit 12:8–9).[12] In the
third century, Cyprian, the bishop of Carthage, wrote, "Fre-
quently apply yourself to almsgiving, whereby souls are freed
from death."[13]

Therefore almsgiving is almost sacramental, an outward and
visible sign of one's gratitude to God. It is a way of thanking
God for his love by giving love to others, a kind of "paying it
forward." Since the members of the Church came from all social

classes, it was within the Church that many wealthy converts were directly confronted with the face of poverty, including those widows and orphans who might otherwise be homeless and starving without the support of the Church community. Christians of all social classes came to understand that unity in the body of Christ meant not only a unity with Christ, but also a unity with one another in Christ. And this meant that each Christian had a responsibility to care about, and care for, their brothers and sisters in the Lord. Those with more shared with those who had less, in imitation of the apostles in the book of Acts.

But, as we have seen, it also became clear that the gifts of God were not meant to be kept for the Church only; they were to be shared beyond the boundaries of the Church, in the wider community. And this is where Christianity's revolution of charity became even more radical. Christians helped non-Christians—they gave to those outside of their own circle—something unheard of in the ancient world. In the fourth century, the emperor Julian "the Apostate" admitted that Christian charity embarrassed the pagans because it benefited non-Christians. As he tried in vain to bring back paganism, he bemoaned the fact that outside the Church, he could not get people to be so selfless.

Even more amazing, given the cultural context, was that the Christian religion made caring for the poor a part of their ritual. From the beginning of the Church's existence, at each worship service a collection was taken up for the less fortunate (see 1 Corinthians 16:1–3). The word *Eucharist* means "thanksgiving," and it seems to have been assumed that Christians would not express their gratitude to God in the Mass without also making some provision for God's people who were in need. In the middle of the second century, the Christian philosopher Saint Justin Martyr wrote a defense of the faith in which he described to his pagan audience exactly what it is that Christians do in their worship services. There we read that liturgy was remarkably like what it is to this day. Specifically, Justin explains, "they who are well to do, and willing, give what each thinks fit, and what is collected is deposited with the presider, who helps the orphans and widows and those who, through sickness or any other cause, are in need, and those who are in prison and the strangers sojourning among us, and in a word takes care of all who are in need."[14]

It was the job of the deacons to distribute the offerings to those in need, whether those offerings were in the form of money or very often in the form of other resources, such as food or clothing. The widows of the churches were charged with keeping the bishops informed about who was going without basic necessities, and the bishops directed the deacons to distribute the resources as needed. Eventually, the popes set up "deacon stations" in Rome, specific churches where the poor could come to receive food, clothing, or even find a safe place to sleep in the portico. The feasts of the martyrs were special occasions when the poor were invited to a meal. These churches became the first food pantries, soup kitchens, and even homeless shelters. Some of the early deacon stations were in churches one can visit today if one goes to Rome, including the churches of Santi Cosma e Damiano, and Santa Maria in Cosmedin.[15]

Church offerings were also used to free slaves and to release the innocent from prison (or at least bribe the guards to provide

better treatment). By the third century, a letter of Pope Corne-
lius (bishop of Rome 251–253) mentions that the Christians of
Rome were supporting fifteen hundred widows, orphans, and
other needy people.[16] This means that a church with a membership that has been estimated at ten thousand to thirty thousand
members was supporting anywhere from 5 to 15 percent of its
members solely on the donations of its wealthier members—
and this doesn't even include what the Church was doing to
minister to its non-Christian neighbors. Eventually, the Church
would literally invent such things as orphanages (so that the
poor would have an alternative to exposing infants and leaving
them to die), hostels (for pilgrimages), and hospitals.[17] During
times of plague, when even the *doctors* got out of town to avoid
infection, Christians cared for the sick, even the non-Christian
sick, and at the risk of their own lives.[18]

Finally, the Church made sure that the poor received a
proper burial. Roman funeral clubs provided burial for their
members but required the payment of dues, which meant that
the poorest folks were left out. Those who could not afford
funeral expenses were buried in mass graves. But the Church
took care of the poorest of the poor since the wealthy paid for,
and even provided space for, the burial of the poor in their
community. It is no coincidence that Christians tended to leave
titles of nobility off their grave markers, since they believed
that those who die in Christ are all equals.

Roman society was built on relationships of reciprocity.
Wealthy patrons helped their "clients" with the expectation that
the clients would return the favor by adding to the prestige of
the patron. This could mean anything from following the patron

around town as part of his entourage to doing the patron's dirty work for him. A patron would not give anything to anyone who was not in a position to give something in return. Giving was, in a word, selfish. Over the course of time, pagan Romans were embarrassed that the Church had become the patron of the poor, but without the usual expectations of reciprocation. The only expectation was prayers of intercession. The recipients were told who had contributed to their support, so that they could pray for their benefactors by name. Thus both rich and poor had a ministry. There was a reward for giving, but it was not a reward that held any value according to the priorities of the world. The reward was bound up with the hope of eternal life, and thus the focus was on the eternal—storing up treasure in heaven.

With the legalization of Christianity in the fourth century, Roman philanthropy was gradually changed to conform to the model of Christian charity, and in some cases the Church's role in relation to the poor was even written into law.[19]

Honor and Shame

There were strong class divisions in Roman culture, and even though some upward mobility was possible (even for freed slaves), that phenomenon only intensified the conviction that one deserved one's station in life. If people prospered, they had earned it. If people were *fortunate,* it meant that Fortune (a pagan goddess) had favored them for some reason. On the other hand, if someone was unfortunate, there was probably a reason for that as well. But the explanation often had less to do with an individual's behavior and more to do with that person's family of origin (or situation of origin, in the case of a slave or orphan). This means that, for the most part, people assumed that both wealth and poverty were—and should be—hereditary.[20]

Those with abundance came from abundance, and that was as it should be—at least that's what the wealthy believed. They deserved what they had, and they deserved to be the ones with all the power. Roman writers argued that the rich were naturally the best politicians because they were more trustworthy than the poor: because they were rich, they didn't need to steal!

A person's place in society was determined by where his or her family was in the ranks of honor. The more wealthy and powerful, the more honorable. The less wealthy and powerful, the less honorable. One of the worst things that could happen to an upper-class person was to lose honor. To be shamed was ruinous to the powerful. But fortunately for them, or so they thought, they had a way out. Suicide. The Romans believed that suicide was a legitimate, and often the best, option for those who suffered shame. Famous suicides include Brutus (one of Julius Caesar's assassins), the philosopher Seneca (the emperor Nero "advised" him to kill himself), and the emperor Nero (he tried to kill himself but ultimately ordered someone else to kill him). The Church rejected the idea of hereditary honor, and it also rejected suicide as an antidote to humiliation.[21]

Ironically, or perhaps understandably, the shame that wealthy and powerful Romans feared became a source of entertainment for them. Criminals were executed publicly and in very humiliating ways. And the plays in the theaters made mockery and humiliation a form of comedy. Roman society was a gossip-driven culture, to the point where the honor of one family was often enhanced through the shame of another. The leaders of the Church repeatedly tried to discourage Christians from attending such shows, though they were not always successful. But to the extent that Christians refused to take part in the humiliation of their fellow human beings, especially when this activity was engaged in as a form of sport, they were seen as antisocial. This was one of the justifications for the persecution of Christians; and their humiliation and death in the arena furnished entertainment for the masses.

Conclusions and Consequences

In affirming selfless giving and affirming the poor as worthy of charity (love), the Church rejected the ancient world's assumption that poverty was the fault of the poor. The Church corrected that worldview, providing new perspectives: that there is no hierarchy of humanity; that some people are not more worthy of respect than others, and that a person's prosperity (or lack thereof) is not a demonstration of their worth. All are equal in the eyes of God. To be humble is not a sin, since Christ humbled himself (Philippians 2:6–7). What is a sin is hoarding resources and showing favoritism to the rich. Jesus condemned such behavior as self-serving (Luke 14:7–14).

The Church also refused to go to the other extreme; it rejected the idea that to be wealthy was a sin in and of itself.[22] Thus the Church would have none of the false dichotomy of the heretics who pitted the spirit against the material world but yielded the same result that we have seen among the pagans: justification for ignoring the poor.[23] The Christians rejected the either-or approach of the two extremes in favor of a middle way: neither expecting a utopia built by a perfected humanity nor throwing up their hands in despair over human depravity, the Church set standards for morality and then offered forgiveness and reconciliation when people failed to live up to those standards. Therefore, as we have seen, Christianity is not to be completely social with little or no personal faith, nor is it to be completely individualistic without engagement with the world. Rather, it incorporates a balance of individual faith commitment with social responsibility.

For the Christians, to be in the world (but not of the world) meant cooperating with God's activity. While Roman laws, and even Roman philanthropy, were designed to preserve and solidify distinctions of social class, Christian charity diminished those distinctions, in the spirit of Galatians 3:28, and gave the people of the world a sense of obligation to care for those who were less fortunate.[24] Christian generosity also included forgiving others and loving one's enemy.

As the only religion to promote the human rights of everyone, even those outside of its boundaries, Christianity was unprecedented in teaching that religion had both the right and the duty to critique the behavior of others in order to protect the weak and innocent. Of course this critique got Christians in trouble within their pagan culture, and it is part of the reason they were persecuted. But the Christians believed they could not do otherwise, based on their conviction that the value of a human being does not rest on their membership in a particular group, or their ability to contribute to the public welfare. Rather that value is universal, and every person is owed respect regardless of their standing in society. Furthermore, this conviction was not something that humans discovered for themselves—it was revealed by God, in the teachings and ministry of Jesus Christ and his apostles.

By rejecting the separation of the haves and have-nots, the Church rejected the divisiveness of class distinctions and class envy and promoted a unity that transcended social status and economic differences. The message to the wealthy was: Do not congratulate yourself for your accomplishments—much less for your accumulations—but rather give thanks to God by giving of your surplus to those who have less. The poor are your best investment.

Thus the Church changed the world by the values it rejected. The Church rejected the idea that poverty was the fault of the poor, and it rejected the idea that everyone deserved their station in life. The wealthy and powerful could no longer justify ignoring the poor. The Church rejected the idea that honor and shame were hereditary, and it rejected suicide as a remedy for the loss of honor. The Church rejected the use of humiliation and death as forms of entertainment. And it rejected the moral relativism of a culture that often claimed that morals were culturally conditioned, and that ultimately behavior was a matter of personal preference. The Church—even before it could legally own anything—became the distributor of alms and inadvertently (and ironically) shamed Roman society into eventually accepting its obligation to care for all human beings. In short, the Church rejected those aspects of ancient culture that caused divisions among people and perpetuated artificial distinctions that devalued some people for the benefit (and entertainment) of others.

As the same time, the Church changed the world by what it affirmed: the obligation of the powerful to protect the weak. This is one of the primary ways that humans cooperate with the work of God, and the grace of God, in the world. As we have now seen, a world without Christianity would be a world without food pantries, soup kitchens, homeless shelters, orphanages, hostels, hospice, or even hospitals. A world without Christianity would be a world in which people did only what they thought was best for themselves.

Finally, Christians were not afraid to let it be known that what they did they did because of their relationship with God in Christ, and that their charity was the fruit of their faith (Matthew 5:14–16). Thus as they ministered to the sick during times of plague, and as the astonished pagans wondered at their motives, those who witnessed—and those who recovered—often converted, being convinced that Christians had a perspective that went beyond this life. Their faith was bigger than life, and they would risk their lives to live their faith, because they knew that eternal life awaited them. So charity became evangelization, and the world would never be the same, because the Christians followed Jesus's command to love their neighbors.

CHAPTER 7

A REVOLUTION IN DEATH

The Conquest of the Last Enemy

The last enemy to be destroyed is death." That was what Saint Paul told the Corinthians (1 Corinthians 15:26). We believe in the *resurrection*—not just the immortality of the soul, but the resurrection of the body. That idea marked the difference between the Christians and their pagan neighbors. A dead body was something a pagan didn't want to think about. The mere sight of a corpse made a pagan ritually unclean, not to mention giving him the willies. Yet Christians treated dead bodies as though they were worth something—as though they were still somehow connected to the honored dead, not just a cast-off container for the soul.

The account of the martyrdom of Saint Polycarp of Smyrna tells us what happened after he died.

> But when the adversary of the race of the righteous, the envious, malicious, and wicked one, saw how impressive his martyrdom was, and how blamelessly he had lived from the beginning, and how he was now crowned with the wreath of immortality, having beyond dispute received his reward, he did his best to make sure we could

not take away the least memorial of him, although many desired to do this, and to keep fellowship with his holy flesh. For this end he suggested to Nicetes, the father of Herod and brother of Alce, to go and beg the governor not to give up his body to be buried. "Otherwise," he said, "they might forsake the crucified one and begin to worship this one." . . .

The centurion, then, seeing the strife excited by the Jews, placed the body in the midst of the fire, and it was burned up. Therefore we later took up his bones, which we regarded as more precious than the most exquisite jewels, and purer than gold. We put them in an appropriate place, and there, when we are gathered together (if we have the chance) with joy and rejoicing, the Lord shall grant us to celebrate the birthday of his martyrdom, both in memory of those who have already finished their course, and for the exercising and preparation of those yet to walk in their steps.[1]

This is the first full account we have of a Christian martyrdom outside the Bible, and we see that the Christians were very much interested in the physical remains of the martyr— his relics. Polycarp's friends almost laughed at the suggestion that they would turn from worshipping Christ to worshipping Polycarp—only someone completely ignorant of Christian belief could suggest that. But they entombed what few remains they could recover "in an appropriate place"—which meant a place where they could meet on the anniversary of Polycarp's death and celebrate his feast day. Notice, too, that the word they used for "anniversary" is literally "birthday"—they celebrated Polycarp's birth into eternal life.

We also notice that, in collecting Polycarp's remains, Polycarp's friends did not think they were doing something that was *necessary* for Polycarp's good. There's no indication that they thought Polycarp would be any worse off because his body was burned to ashes. They didn't even seem to believe that he would be any worse off if they hadn't collected his bones.

But *they* would be worse off. The reason they give for wanting to collect the relics of Polycarp is that they wanted "to keep fellowship with his holy flesh."

The idea of "holy flesh" would have made no sense to a pagan philosopher, but it made perfect sense to a Christian. We were created in the image of God, and the Son of God himself took flesh. He gave his flesh for food, which in the Eucharist is assimilated to the flesh of every Christian.

That makes the body more than a sort of envelope for the soul, a container that is cast off at death. When we Christians speak of the dignity of the body, we mean that the human person is composed of body and soul. The body is holy because we were made in the image of God, because God became one of us, and because our bodies are united to the flesh and blood of God in Christ.

When we read the accounts of Christ's burial in the Gospels, we see that his followers treated his body with reverence. Joseph of Arimathea had to "take courage" to give Jesus the tomb he thought he deserved—just asking Pilate for the body might brand Joseph as another seditious criminal. But Joseph did it because it was what ought to be done.

And when evening had come, since it was the day of Preparation, that is, the day before the Sabbath, Joseph of Arimathea, a respected member of the council, who was also himself looking for the kingdom of God, took courage and went to Pilate, and asked for the body of Jesus. And Pilate wondered if he were already dead; and summoning the centurion, he asked him whether he was already dead. And when he learned from the centurion that he was dead, he granted the body to Joseph. And he bought a linen shroud, and taking him down, wrapped him in the linen shroud, and laid him in a tomb which had been hewn out of the rock; and he rolled a stone against the door of the tomb. Mary Magdalene and Mary the mother of Joses saw where he was laid.

And when the Sabbath was past, Mary Magdalene, and Mary the mother of James, and Salome, bought spices, so that they might go and anoint him. (Mark 15:42–16:1)

Of course, we know what happened when they got there: they found no body to anoint. John gives us a partial eyewitness account:

Now on the first day of the week Mary Magdalene came to the tomb early, while it was still dark, and saw that the stone had been taken away from the tomb. So she ran, and went to Simon Peter and the other disciple, the one whom Jesus loved, and said to them, "They have taken the Lord out of the tomb, and we do not know

where they have laid him." Peter then came out with
the other disciple, and they went toward the tomb. They
both ran, but the other disciple outran Peter and reached
the tomb first; and stooping to look in, he saw the linen
cloths lying there, but he did not go in. Then Simon Peter
came, following him, and went into the tomb; he saw the
linen cloths lying, and the napkin, which had been on his
head, not lying with the linen cloths but rolled up in a
place by itself. Then the other disciple, who reached the
tomb first, also went in, and he saw and believed; for as
yet they did not know the scripture, that he must rise
from the dead. (John 20:1–9)

The little detail that the head cloth was "rolled up in a
place by itself" is telling. Like all the Gospel writers, John is
very economical with details: he reports only what he thinks
is important and significant. According to John (21:20, 24), the
author of this Gospel was "the other disciple, the one whom
Jesus loved," so he is telling us what he remembers having seen
himself when he went in after Peter. It stuck in his memory
that the head cloth was rolled up neatly in a corner away from
the other cloths. That detail tells us something about Christ. It
suggests that Christ had real appreciation for the people who
had reverence for his body: he was careful with their work, not
ripping the cloths off but carefully removing them and deposit-
ing them neatly.

The first Christian martyr after Christ was Stephen, and
we read that after his death "devout men buried Stephen, and
made great lamentation over him" (Acts 8:2). Just as they did

with Christ, the Christians took care that Stephen's body was reverently treated.

All this probably sounds quite ordinary to us. We have a huge industry devoted to making sure that the bodies of our loved ones are neatly dressed before burial. But we have to understand what a shocking, and really loathsome, idea this would have been to most of the people in the ancient Roman world.

The Riddle of Death

Death was the riddle the pagans couldn't solve. What happened when people died? There might be life after life, or there might not be. If there was, it might be something pleasant, or it might be only eternal gloom, even for the virtuous.

Gloom was what Homer saw, and Homer was the closest thing the pagans had to a Sacred Scripture. Homer was the author most essential to any curriculum in the Greek-speaking world—and in the upper classes of Roman society, where Greek occupied the same place as the universal language of culture that Latin occupied during the Renaissance. So Homer's idea of the afterlife counted for something.

In the *Odyssey*, Odysseus visits the realm of the dead in Hades and meets the great men who fell in the Trojan War. These were not the evil wretches whose misdeeds litter history; these were the exemplars of Greek heroism. And what has Achilles to say about death?

Renown'd Ulysses! think not death a theme
Of consolation; I had rather live
The servile hind for hire, and eat the bread
Of some man scantily himself sustain'd,
Than sov'reign empire hold o'er all the shades.[2]

Homer puts these words in the mouth of one of his characters, but they seem to represent a common Greek belief. Other Greek writers give us the same idea, or worse. Death was rotten even if you were a famous hero; better to be a poor laborer hired by a poor farmer than to be dead. Under those circumstances, death was certainly not something to look forward to. The best that could be said was that it might sometimes be better than the alternative. The well-educated Roman patriot might say, with Horace, *Dulce et decorum est pro patria mori* (It is sweet and proper to die for one's country), but that was probably because he believed that death meant simple annihilation, which was preferable to living in dishonor. The philosophical pagan strove to accept death as inevitable, often by persuading himself that life was unbearable anyway, and not existing was better than existing. The ordinary working-class pagan followed every superstitious ritual that might possibly postpone death a little longer.

Naturally, one thing a Roman couldn't abide was a dead body. Cremation was the normal Roman funeral practice: it got rid of the dead body quickly, and (at least if you were lucky) it kept the spirit of the deceased from coming back to haunt you.

Perhaps the worst thing about burying the dead was that it

was likely to attract spiritual infestations. Roman popular culture was grossly superstitious. Even an educated Roman gentleman who in the light of noon laughed at the superstitious rabble was scared to death of ghosts at midnight. Since no one knew what happened after death, the superstitious imagination ran riot. Graves were places where ghosts might congregate, and who knew what a ghost might do to you if you met one on a dark and stormy night. Christians, on the other hand, have a definite understanding of what happens after death. And to the educated pagan, what Christians believed must have sounded a bit mad.

Christians believe in the resurrection of the body—we say that every time we recite the Creed, but we seldom think what an odd thing it appears to be. Some (not all) pagan philosophers thought that the soul was immortal; they saw the body as a machine animated by the soul and dead without it. But it simply never occurred to pagans to talk about the resurrection of the body.

Yet the Christian religion depends upon this idea. Christ's resurrection is the pattern for ours. This is what Saint Paul told the Corinthians:

> *Now if Christ is preached as raised from the dead, how can some of you say that there is no resurrection of the dead? But if there is no resurrection of the dead, then Christ has not been raised; if Christ has not been raised, then our preaching is in vain and your faith is in vain. We are even found to be misrepresenting God, because we testified of God that he raised Christ, whom he did*

*not raise if it is true that the dead are not raised. For if
the dead are not raised, then Christ has not been raised.
If Christ has not been raised, your faith is futile and you
are still in your sins. Then those also who have fallen
asleep in Christ have perished. If for this life only we
have hoped in Christ, we are of all men most to be pitied.*

*But in fact Christ has been raised from the dead,
the first fruits of those who have fallen asleep. For as
by a man came death, by a man has come also the resurrection of the dead. For as in Adam all die, so also
in Christ shall all be made alive. But each in his own
order: Christ the first fruits, then at his coming those
who belong to Christ. (1 Corinthians 15:12-23)*

For Christians, the body is integral to the person, and the
person will have a body for eternity. This doesn't mean that it
will be identical to the body we have now. Polycarp's friends
were not worried for Polycarp's sake that his body was burned
to ashes; they knew he would live again in a glorified body—
one that bears the same relation to our earthly body that the
mature plant bears to the seed. Saint Paul explained this idea:

*But some one will ask, "How are the dead raised? With
what kind of body do they come?" You foolish man!
What you sow does not come to life unless it dies. And
what you sow is not the body which is to be, but a bare
kernel, perhaps of wheat or of some other grain. But God
gives it a body as he has chosen, and to each kind of seed
its own body. For not all flesh is alike, but there is one*

kind for men, another for animals, another for birds, and another for fish. There are celestial bodies and there are terrestrial bodies; but the glory of the celestial is one, and the glory of the terrestrial is another. There is one glory of the sun, and another glory of the moon, and another glory of the stars; for star differs from star in glory. So is it with the resurrection of the dead. What is sown is perishable, what is raised is imperishable. It is sown in dishonor, it is raised in glory. It is sown in weakness, it is raised in power. It is sown a physical body, it is raised a spiritual body. (1 Corinthians 15:35-44)

This is the reason for what must sometimes seem like a strangely ambivalent attitude toward the body among Christians. On the one hand, it doesn't really matter what happens to the body—the resurrection will happen anyway. On the other hand, the body really is part of the person, and as such deserves reverent treatment.

Wherever the Church spread, Christians took up the practice of burying their dead. The first major building projects of the new faith in Rome were not churches—one never knew when the next persecution might break out, and the building would be knocked to the ground. The first visible Christian structures were the catacombs.

In the catacombs the Christians buried their dead and celebrated the "birthdays" of the martyrs. They surrounded their loved ones with the most elaborate and costly art they could afford—sometimes mere graffiti, but in some cases they produced some of the most striking paintings that have survived from ancient times. The more martyrs there were, the more often Christians assembled in the catacombs.

The catacombs were quite visible constructions—you can't dig out a system of tunnels, with masons and architects and artists all contributing to the work, without people knowing about it. The pagans noticed. They couldn't help noticing. The Roman catacombs eventually extended to more than sixty miles of labyrinthine underground corridors. Estimates of the population of this "city of the dead" range into the millions. And Christians, understandably, became known as the people who handled dead bodies—who polluted themselves at graves.

Yet there must have been something attractive about the Christian way of burial. It exercised a strong fascination, perhaps because it confronted Romans' worst fears. Christians were the people who dug graves and handled bodies, so they were the people who had no fear of death. The courage of the martyrs was a billboard advertisement for Christianity, but it may be that the courage of the Christian *fossores*—the "Diggers"—was almost as impressive. Confronted with death, Christians refused to look the other way. They celebrated the martyrs' death, because they knew the answer to the riddle.

The Status of Corpses

In spite of all their indulgence of the body, pagans had little respect for it. A pagan might see beauty, and admire it, in the human body. But he knew that the beauty was temporary. It was a transient phenomenon, and the philosopher knew better than to be led astray by it. The soul was what mattered, and so the body was worthless except as a home for the soul.

It is hard for us to imagine the superstitious horror that dead bodies evoked in even the most enlightened pagans. Julian the Apostate, the emperor who tried to turn back the tide of Christianity and revive paganism as the state religion, could not abide the very public funerals that were taking place in Antioch.

> *We have heard that dead corpses are carried to interment through large crowds of people and numerous spectators, a sight that defiles the eyes of men by its inauspicious appearance. For what day is well-omened by a funeral? And how can we afterwards approach the gods and the temples?*[3]

Julian often berated the Christians for what he saw as their ignorant superstition, but the only good reason he could give for prohibiting public funerals—which is what he did—was that the sight of a body brought bad luck. And, of course, bodies polluted a person ritually, so that they couldn't serve the pagan gods in their temples. Even *seeing* a funeral procession was enough to render a good pagan impure, in need of some serious cleansing before he could bring his sacrifices to the gods.

But the people of Antioch had changed their minds by this time. Julian was—or was trying to be—the voice of Roman tradition, but the voice of the people had spoken in favor of funeral processions down the main street.

We find that, as time went on, even *pagan* fashions were changing. The Diggers had started something, and the work of burial—the thing that made them strange and horrible to their neighbors—started to become a bit of a fad among the pagans, too. As we head into the fourth century, we see that more and more pagans were buried rather than cremated.

Was it the example of the Christians and Jews that changed the fashion? We don't have enough evidence to prove such a theory either way. But the fact is that the catacombs had made the Christians odd in the Roman world—and then a century later pagans were following the Christian lead and burying their own dead. We can at least say that Christians were ahead of the trend. Perhaps the Christians really were teaching the rest of the world to overcome the horror of death.

By the late 300s, a new attitude toward the dead had spread throughout the empire. When Saint Ambrose, the bishop of Milan, had a new basilica put up in that city, the people begged him to consecrate it with the relics of martyrs. He obliged them by looking for some local martyrs to dig up and transfer to the new church. We have his story of what happened in a letter he wrote to his sister Marcellina, who by that time had become a nun.

I want to make sure that nothing that happens here while you are away escapes the knowledge of your holiness, so you must know that we have found some bodies of holy martyrs. After I had dedicated the basilica, many people came to me and said, as if one mouth, "Consecrate this one the way you did the Roman basilica." And I answered, "I certainly will, if I find any relics of martyrs." And at once a kind of prophetic ardor seemed to enter my heart. Why should I use many words? God favored us, for even the clergy were afraid who were bidden to clear away the earth from the spot before the chancel screen of Saints Felix and Nabor. I found the appropriate signs, and when we brought in some people on whom hands were to be laid, the power of the holy martyrs became so clear, that even while I was still silent, one was seized and thrown prostrate at the holy burial-place. We found two men of marvelous stature, such as those of ancient days. All the bones were perfect, and there was much blood. During the whole of those two days there was an enormous concourse of people. Briefly we arranged the whole in order, and as evening was now coming on transferred them to the basilica of Fausta, where watch was kept during the night, and some received the laying on of hands. On the following day we translated the relics to the basilica called Ambrosian. During the translation a blind man was healed.[4]

Ambrose was writing not long after Julian's brief attempt to swing the empire back to paganism—and see what a difference the Christian attitude toward death makes. Julian would be disgusted just by seeing a funeral procession in the street; he'd have to go home and wash himself, and he'd be ritually impure for a day. Ambrose rejoices at finding two dead bodies—and the whole city of Milan rejoices with him. Instead of fearing ritual impurity, the people attribute miracles to the relics of the saints. Unearthing the martyrs' remains is an occasion of joy for the whole population, and for Ambrose himself, who can't wait to write a letter to his sister about it.

Christians honor the dead because the body is a tangible

connection to the person, who is still living. The body is also *evidence,* concrete proof that the person actually existed. And that, too, is a distinctively Christian phenomenon. The pagan heroes were the stuff of myths; Christians based their whole faith on facts of history. Luke goes out of his way to date the nativity of Christ in his Gospel, and the martyrdom stories— like Polycarp's—are often compiled using actual public records from the martyrs' trials. When Constantine made Christianity legal, there was a sudden fad for pilgrimages to the tombs of the martyrs and other historic Christian sites—a fad started by Constantine's mother, Helena, who practically invented archaeology in her search for the cross of Christ. History matters to Christians.

Care for the Dead

So far we've talked about how Christians honored the body in death. Yet we also know that Christians never thought this honor was *necessary* to the well-being of the dead. It was something Christians did to show reverence for the departed and for the God who had made them in his image. So we find an interesting ambivalence in the way the early Christians thought about the bodies of the dead. On the one hand, it was appropriate to show honor to the body. On the other hand, it didn't really matter what happened to it.

How can we make sense of that seeming contradiction? It's not really contradictory at all. The honor we show to the bodies of the saints is something we do for ourselves, not for them.

One of the most affecting scenes in Saint Augustine's *Confessions* is the death of his mother Monica. There is nothing in classical literature like it: a man who mourns the loss of his mother, not only because she is his mother, but because she was a fountain of wisdom. Monica was the steady rock in the family while her young son ran off and experimented with every fashionable idea, and her joy was complete when he returned to the Catholic faith of his mother. Augustine, in turn, was devoted to his mother.

Augustine was born and grew up in Africa, but he made his career in Italy as a teacher. Monica followed him to Italy. In Milan, where Augustine was teaching, she met Ambrose, and by Ambrose's patient friendship Augustine was brought back to the Catholic faith. After his conversion, Augustine and his mother and brother were on their way back to Africa; but when Monica and her two sons were in the port city of Ostia, she fell ill. Saint Augustine wrote:

> *One day, being very sick, she swooned away, and was for a little while insensible. We ran in, but she soon came to herself again, and looking upon me and my brother that were standing by her, said to us (as if she were genuinely curious), "Where have I been?"*
>
> *Then, seeing us struck with grief, she said, "Here you shall bury your mother."*
>
> *I held my peace, and kept from weeping; but my brother said something to the effect that he wished—as if it were a happier thing—that she might not die abroad, but in her own country.*

When she heard that, concern showed on her face
that he should have such notions, and she stopped him
with her eyes. Looking at me, she said, "Do you hear
what he says?" Then to us both, "Lay this body any-
where. Don't worry about that. Only I beg of you that,
wherever you are, you will make remembrance of me at
the Lord's altar."

And when she had expressed her mind to us with
such words as she could, she said no more, but lay strug-
gling with her disease, which was growing worse.[5]

Monica—we know her as Saint Monica now—is a very good example of that ambivalence about the body that we have been talking about. On the one hand, the body is unimportant. God will raise us on the last day with a glorified body, and it makes absolutely no difference if we've been burned to ashes like Polycarp. But, on the other hand, the body is a visible, tangible connection with the Christian who is still living. Monica was buried at Ostia, far from home: her sons followed her wishes and didn't worry about getting her back to Africa. So her body was unimportant. But her relics are in Rome now, venerated by countless thousands of pilgrims every year. So her body is very important indeed. Augustine sets out to address this apparent contradiction in his book *On the Care of the Dead.* There he answers questions regarding the body, explaining that it is not important yet very important; he does not worry at all about burial yet advises that the bodies of the dead be treated with honor. He begins with the cases of horrible massacres, where the dead are never buried.

In a pile of butchered bodies like that, could they not even be buried? Pious faith does not even dread this very much. We believe what is foretold, that not even ravening beasts will keep their bodies from rising: not a hair of their heads shall perish. Truth himself would certainly not say, "do not fear those who kill the body but cannot kill the soul" [Matthew 10:28], if anything enemies might decide to do to the bodies of the slain could stand in the way of the life to come. No one would be so absurd as to contend that we should not fear that they will kill the body before death, but we should fear that they might not bury the body after death! . . .

So, then, all these things—care of funeral, placement in a tomb, pomp of ceremonies—are more for comfort of the living than for help to the dead. If it did the ungodly any good to have costly tombs, it would harm the godly to have poor or no tomb. In human eyes, that rich man who was clad in purple was given a lavish funeral by his household—but how much more lavish a funeral that poor man who was full of sores was given by the ministry of angels, who bore him not out into a marble tomb, but up into Abraham's bosom![6]

This is one side of the coin: Christians have no need to worry about what happens to the body. Nothing that can happen will harm our chances of resurrection.

But there is another side:

Yet it does not follow that the bodies of the departed are to be despised and flung aside—and certainly not the

*bodies of the just and faithful. Their spirits used those
bodies as organs and vessels of all good works.*

*For if a father's garment and ring, and anything else
he wore, is the more dear to those who are left behind the
greater their affection is towards their parents, then the
bodies themselves are certainly not to be spurned, which
truly we wear more familiarly and closer than anything
we put on. For the bodies are not some kind of ornament
or tool put on from outside, but they have to do with the
very nature of man. . . .*

*If this is true, then doubtless it is also true that pro-
viding a place for the interment of bodies at the memorials of saints is a mark of a good human affection towards
the remains of one's friends—since, if there is religion in
the burying, there cannot help being religion in thinking
about where the burying should be. But while it is desir-
able there should be comforts like these for the survivors,
to demonstrate their pious mind towards their beloved,
I do not see what helps they are to the dead except in
this way: that when they remember of the place where
the bodies of those whom they love are deposited, they
should by prayer commend them to those same saints,
who have as patrons taken them into their charge to
aid them before the Lord. Which indeed they would be
still able to do, even if they were not able to inter them
in such places. But then the only reason why the name*
memorials *or* monuments *is given to those tombs of the
dead which become specially distinguished, is that they
recall them to* memory, *and make us think about those*

who by death are withdrawn from the eyes of the living,
so that they may not by forgetfulness be also withdrawn
from our hearts.[7]

Our reverence for the bodies of the departed is not pointless. It reminds us of our still living connection with all who have ever lived. Augustine exulted when the relics of the martyr Saint Stephen were transferred to his diocese. *We believe in the communion of saints,* as the Creed reminds us. If we bury our dead near the memorial of a saint, then we remember to ask that saint to pray for them, and to pray for us. The walls of the catacombs—and tombs throughout the ancient Christian world—bear abundant testimony to the interrelationship of Christians living on earth with those living in heaven. Chiseled inscriptions and scrawled graffiti communicate the same common pleas for the intercession of the saints.

Patronage

The idea that a saint can be a "patron" is so familiar to us that we probably never think about what the word means. This is a fascinating example of how early Christians saw through the barrier of death. The fact that we still have a connection with the saints who have gone before us, that their prayers can do us good, was interpreted by the Roman Christians in a particularly Roman way. They imagined it as being very much like the "patronage" system that permeated Roman society.

In Rome, an ambitious man, or one who just wanted to get

along in society without too much trouble, would attach himself as a *client* to a *patron*—usually a man who was richer than he was. The relationship was good for both parties.

The client had the rich man's support in the law courts—it would be very dishonorable for a patron to see his client suffering any preventable injustice. If the client was in financial trouble, the patron would bail him out. The patron welcomed the client into the extended family as a sort of auxiliary member, one who could take his (suitably humble) place at family worship. The more clients a rich man had, the better he was thought of in society. The client was expected to support his patron if he ran for political office, and stand with his patron if his patron was having trouble with some other rich and powerful person.

This system gave Christians a perfect model for understanding their relationship with the saints. The saint was rich: he possessed all that heaven had to offer. By placing themselves under the protection of a saint as a patron, the Christians could hope for a good hearing in heaven's court. If they were in trouble, they would ask the saint to intercede for them with almighty God. The ancient homilies and graffiti tell us what Christian clients sought from their heavenly patrons: the cure of a child, the safe return of a traveling spouse, deliverance from an oppressor.

We no longer think of the world in terms of the client-patron system of ancient Rome, but Catholics still use that word *patron* to describe their relationship with a favorite saint.

And here we have the real completion of the Christian revolution: victory over death. Pagans ran screaming from ghosts; Christians ran for comfort to saints.

The Last Enemy

"The last enemy to be destroyed is death." The revolution in
the Christian way of death sums up the revolutions in our way
of life. In Christ, the bonds of a loving family continue beyond
death. Human beings have dignity, even when their bodies are
decomposing. And even the work of diggers and corpse handlers
has become a holy task. The position of the *fossores,* the Diggers
of the catacombs, was considered an ecclesiastical office.

Once upon a time, bodies were buried far outside the walls
of great cities like Rome. Today, Rome's most prominent monuments, its Christian basilicas, stand over the grave sites of
the apostles—and even the Colosseum is preserved primarily
because Christians died there.

Yet all those who died still live today, and they keep
fellowship—they keep communion—with the Church on earth.

CHAPTER 8

A REVOLUTION OF THE STATE

Religious Freedom

M any, if not most, people think that the concept of religious freedom was invented by the Founding Fathers of the United States, in response to the religious persecution that they (or their ancestors) had experienced in Europe. Some, perhaps, believe that the freedom to worship according to one's own conscience was a product of the Enlightenment. Either way, the United States is usually held up as the great pioneer of the right to freedom of worship. But this is not true. What has been called the "American Experiment" was actually originally the Constantinian experiment.[1]

To be clear, the emperor Constantine did not make the Roman Empire Christian. The conversion of the empire was all but done by the time Constantine rose to power, and it was done one person, or one family, at a time. There were already major cities where a significant percentage of the population— and in some cases a majority—was Christian. Because people were willing to die for their faith, either in the arena or by caring for the sick during times of plague, it was clear to the Roman population that the Church offered something greater than the Roman gods could promise—something greater than life itself. So at a time when being a Christian was still illegal and people were still being persecuted for the faith, the Church was well on its way to converting the empire.

Once Constantine became emperor, one of the first things he did was to legalize Christianity. Many people wrongly believe that Constantine then turned the tables on the former persecutors, made Christianity the only legal religion of the empire, and forced pagans to convert to Christianity. This could not be further from the truth. Constantine did none of these things. In fact, he enacted a law that guaranteed freedom of religion for all citizens.

Our seventh revolution is a revolution of the state—a revolution of government itself, in which citizenship would not determine religious loyalties and people were free to worship according to their own conscience. But before we get to that, we have to look at what government was like before the Church converted the empire.

What Is Government?

What does it mean for a people to be governed? In the ancient world, it meant that some people led and ruled over others on the basis of their claim to a natural right to do so. Certain families, or certain classes of families, had (at some point in the hazy past) risen to the top of the social hierarchy, and they claimed superiority over those whom they ruled. In some cultures, such as the Egyptian and Akkadian, rulers claimed to be divine, extending the social hierarchy into the realm of the gods—as if the hierarchy of humanity was linked with a hierarchy of divinity, and the ruling family was in between humanity and the gods. On this basis they claimed a divine right to rule and placed themselves above all human laws. Whenever rulers claimed their right to rule based on a natural distinction between themselves and their subjects—that is, they claimed that they were better by nature—it was assumed that leadership must be hereditary, to "keep it in the family," so to speak. Those who were not born into the right class could never become leaders, and they usually did not have a voice in the decisions that would affect their lives.[2]

We often think of the government of ancient Greece as an advance over this kind of rule. And it is true that in Greece and Rome, although there was a sharp divide in the classes, there was some possibility of upward mobility from one class to another. Yet this freedom went only so far, and power was all about who had the money. In other words, you could move up the social ladder (and participate in leadership) only by getting rich. But there was a catch. Engaging in business was often frowned upon by those who didn't have to work for a living, so the only really respectable way to acquire wealth was to inherit it, or to "earn" it by conquering in battle and claiming the spoils of war. Therefore, sometimes generals could enter the upper classes by stealing the resources of a conquered people, or by receiving rewards from the emperor for their victories. Otherwise, the wealthy class was mostly made up of old money.

It was usually assumed that the richest people were the best people, the smartest people, and therefore they were the ones with the right to rule. For Plato, the ruling class deserved to rule simply because they were wiser than the rest of the people—but he did not mean to imply that with the right education anyone could rise to the top. What he meant was that only certain people were born to be rulers, and everyone else was born to be ruled. In Plato's dialogue *The Republic,* he described the ideal society, one in which the leaders create the perfect environment for individuals to be good. Plato believed that it is not that individuals choose to be good, and that makes a good society—it is the other way around; the wise few create a perfect society in which the masses have no reason to exercise anything other than good behavior. This is the utilitarian ethic imprinted on a government, and it is based on the assumption that only a select few people are fit to lead. The point is, all of these ancient forms of government are based on the assumption that all people are *not* created equal.

The Romans created their own version of a republic, ruled by a senate and with elected officials. By the time of the birth of Jesus, the Roman Republic had fallen apart because of the aristocracy's greed for power. Julius Caesar had attempted to turn a temporary appointment of emergency leadership into a permanent position of ultimate power—and he was assassinated in 44 BC. The result was a civil war. Soon it became clear that *someone* would emerge as sole ruler; it was just a matter of who it would be. After the decisive Battle of Actium in 31 BC, the Republic disintegrated and Caesar's nephew and adopted heir Octavian assumed power; he became Rome's first emperor and eventually took the name Augustus. Thus, when the republic disintegrated, it became an empire, with Augustus as its first emperor, and with a mission to expand its borders and take over the world. At precisely this time in history, Jesus Christ came and offered an alternative to empire. We call it the *kingdom of God,* but that phrase in Greek could just as well be translated "empire of God." Jesus brought us God's empire and preached it as the Good News—over against the Roman Empire (or any other empire).

Before long, the emperors were not content to have all the power in the world, they wanted divinity as well. Building on the Egyptian custom, Roman emperors began taking divine titles for themselves. Augustus coerced the Senate into proclaiming that his uncle Julius Caesar had become a god after his assassination. And if Caesar was a god, then that meant his heir, his adopted son, was the son of a god. It is important to understand this when one reads in the Gospels that Jesus is called the Son of God. The Scriptures affirm that even though the emperor may claim to be a son of a god, Jesus Christ is *the* Son of *the* God. After Augustus, other emperors started demanding to be called by divine titles, until at the end of the first century the emperor Domitian demanded to be called "lord and god." In the Gospel of John, written about the same time as Domitian's rule, we read that when Saint Thomas saw Jesus in the flesh after the resurrection, and felt his wounds, he confessed his faith in Jesus with the words, "My Lord and my God" (John 20:28).[3] As we will see, Jesus, his apostles, and his Church were offering the world an alternative to rule by power-hungry emperors.

In terms of leadership, one of the biggest problems with dynastic monarchies, republics, and empires was that if you were not from the ruling class, you had no real voice, no participation in shaping your own situation, let alone determining your own future. The belief that certain people had a natural right to rule inevitably led to the belief that everyone else should simply do as they were told. The value of an individual's life was determined by what they could contribute economically to the wealth, and to the wealthy, of the society (as we have seen in a previous chapter). Class-based governments have always assumed that the people of the lower classes exist only for the benefit of the upper classes. Collectively, the ruling class could never do without the laborers who planted and harvested and prepared their food, but as individuals the people of the lower classes were expendable.

The Hebrews knew that rulers were not gods, and that they were not above the law. The stories of the early kings in the Old Testament are evidence of that. Royalty was not equated with divinity, and even the kings were accountable to a higher authority. But in the Judean context, the people could usually, if perhaps naïvely, assume that the king and God were on the same page (the case of David and Bathsheba notwithstanding). And they could also assume that being loyal to the king would not mean being disloyal to God. Even when the kings were not following God, the people had the prophets to try to set them back on the right path.

But this begs the question of what believers are supposed to do when it seems as though they cannot obey both God and their leader(s). What happens when patriotism cannot be reconciled with faithfulness? What happens when one's loyalty is demanded by two opposing powers, and one is forced to choose between empire and kingdom, between Caesar and Christ?

The answer is that one "must obey God rather than men" (Acts 5:29). But this was not an easy thing to do when the earthly rulers held the power to imprison, torture, and put people to death. One of the symbols of the Roman Republic and Empire was called the *fasces,* the bundled rods and axe that warned of the state's power to torture and execute any who were disloyal.

For the Romans, patriotism was so bound up with their religion that they would eventually take to using pagan sacrifices as a test of loyalty. Citizens were required to make a sacrifice in honor of the emperor to prove their patriotism, and refusing to make the sacrifice was considered an act of treason, punishable by death. In times of persecution, this method was used to try to force Christians to deny their faith, and when they would not, they could be exposed, arrested, tortured, and executed.

So what was the Christian response when the empire not only outlawed their religion but declared it treasonous? It was a mixed bag of passive resistance and compliance. Through all the persecutions of the Roman Empire, when Christians were being raped, tortured, dismembered, and murdered— sometimes in front of a cheering crowd—the Church never once took up arms against its oppressors. Resistance was always nonviolent. Christians remembered that Jesus had told them to pray for their persecutors (Matthew 5:44). And when it came time to confront the pagan altars, many (though not all) of the Christians had the courage to refuse to engage in a pagan sacrifice because they knew that God's kingdom was greater than the Roman Empire. The empire could torture and kill, but the kingdom offered something that transcended death—eternal life (Matthew 10:28).

The fact that Christians chose to give up their lives rather than renounce their faith was startling to many pagans. They must have wondered, *What could be more important than life?* The Christians' uncommon determination only demonstrates the revolutionary nature of Christianity as a religion—it is a religion not just for this life; it goes beyond this life and is more important than mortal life itself. What is more, Christians were willing to give their lives (and their livelihoods) not simply to believe something internally, but to practice their faith—they would live the faith, or they would not live at all. Christians took this stand, as the Church rejected the core concepts of ancient government: that all people are not created equal, and that the average person is expendable.

Government as Stewardship

Sometimes it is said that the hierarchy of the Church developed as an imitation of the hierarchy in the Roman government. But this is not true. The hierarchy of the Roman government was a complex combination of the patron-client system with the *cursus honorum,* a standard route of upward career moves meant to propel aristocratic men toward the Senate, or at least as far in that direction as their social status would allow them to go. In other words, the Roman hierarchy was designed to reinforce class distinctions and safeguard the privilege of the wealthy. The hierarchy of the Church, as it was developing, carried no promise of wealth or power; working for the church wasn't even a day job—it was originally a volunteer position.

And while being a leader in the Church certainly would have implied some measure of respect within the Church, in a world where Christians were persecuted, rising to the rank of bishop only put a person on the government's most wanted list.

The hierarchy of the Church developed for reasons other than the promotion of privileged individuals to positions of power. The hierarchy developed so that the traditions of the Church could be passed on to the next generation. This philosophy of leadership influenced the Christian understanding of government: *rulers served the ruled,* not the other way around (see Matthew 20:25–28). In addition to preserving the teachings handed down from Jesus through the apostles, and of course providing and presiding over liturgy, the leaders within the Church were formed into a structure that made it possible for the Church to carry out what Christians understood as their social responsibility.[4] The revolution of community that sprang from the Church's emphasis on love of neighbor and care for the poor led to the need for a system of collection and distribution of money and goods for the needy. The contrast with the Roman Empire could not be more sharp: while the structure of pagan Roman society was designed to serve those at the top, the hierarchical leadership of the Church was meant to serve those at the bottom. Additionally, in the hierarchy of the Church, there was no caste system: anyone—regardless of social standing—could devote his or her life to the service of Christ and his Church, and even a slave could be a bishop.[5]

Within the Church, all people were valued as children of God created in the image of God, regardless of their perceived value to society. Human rights were protected, especially those of the vulnerable, such as the homeless, the disabled, children, and the pre-born. Also, every person was recognized as having free will, as well as the responsibility to exercise that free will within the bounds of Christian morality, and to the end of loving the neighbor. It was believed that everyone should have the freedom to worship according to one's conscience and conviction, rather than being told by the government how (or whom) to worship. And each person had the right, and the duty, to refuse to comply with the government if that meant compromising the faith.

The Christians critiqued Roman culture and government when these failed to protect human rights. The early Christian philosophers (the apologists) were constantly criticizing the morality of the Romans, especially the (perfectly legal) practices of abortion, infanticide, exposure, and the sexual exploitation of children. Some, such as Tertullian, also criticized capital punishment, saying that Christians could not participate in any way in an execution.[6] Most of the early Church Fathers recommended that Christians boycott the blood sports and public executions in the arena. In about the year 177, the Christian apologist Athenagoras wrote, "To see a man put to death is much the same as killing him."[7] In the third century, the Roman priest Novatian wrote, "It is forbidden for us to be spectators of whatever it is forbidden for us to do."[8]

Tertullian also complained that the Romans forced Christians to worship against their will, and, by doing so, took away their freedom.[9] Of course all of this critique may have been counterproductive, since the Romans only escalated the persecution the more they perceived that the Christians were being antisocial. For their part, the Romans hated what they saw as the rigidity of Christians, so that Christian "atheism" was condemned as inflexibility, and ironically this is how the Romans justified their own intolerance and persecution of those who pointed out their immorality.

It may be argued by some that it is unfair to label the behavior of the Romans "immoral," even when they discarded infants and sexually abused children, because these things were for the most part acceptable in their culture. After all, how could they have known better? But to say this is to give in to a cultural relativism that would take away any ability to critique atrocities such as ethnic cleansing and the Holocaust. If the individual Roman did not know any better, it was the gift of the Church, received as revelation from God, that Christianity would teach people a better way—a more humane way.

By the time the Church was in a position to influence government in the fourth century, a Christian idea of government had emerged—that those who governed should be the protectors of those whom they govern. Leadership was not a right; it was a responsibility—one that included serving the "least" of society. To govern was to be entrusted with something very valuable—human beings created in the image of God and the resources to sustain them. In other words, Christian leadership is a form of stewardship.

We can learn something from the story of the martyrdom of Saint Lawrence, who was a deacon of the church of Rome in the third century. In the year 258, Pope Sixtus II, the bishop of Rome, was murdered by imperial guards, and the deacons were rounded up to be executed. The last of the deacons to be arrested was Lawrence. Since the Romans knew that he was in charge of the collection and distribution of the church's offerings, they demanded that he hand over the "treasures of the church." According to the story, he returned with some of the poor of Rome, and said to the authorities, "These are the treasures of the church."[10] Although the story may be embellished a bit, it conveys the attitude of the early Christians. Leadership is service, in which the leaders serve those whom they lead, not the other way around (Matthew 23:11).

As long as Christianity was outlawed, Christian leaders could not do much more than write explanations of the faith (the *apologies*) that provided justifications for Christianity in the hope that the Romans would ease up on the persecution. But these were documents that in all probability were read by more Christians than non-Christians. The Church could influence the empire only one person at a time—through the conversion of individuals. Nevertheless, as Christians lived their faith day by day, they demonstrated to their neighbors their conviction that all people are created in the image of God, and therefore all are created equal. This means that all people are valued—even the weakest who have the least potential for contributing to society—and that no one is expendable. By living in this way, even at the risk of their own lives, the Christians set the stage for the conversion of the empire from pagan to Christian. And eventually this attitude was embraced by one particular convert who would open the door to the conversion of the government itself. That person was the emperor Constantine.

Church and State

At the turn of the fourth century, the Roman state was trying to destroy the Church with its worst persecution ever. In spite of this, the Church was still growing, and the so-called Great Persecution, though brutal, was futile. At this time Constantine arrived on the scene. His mother, now known to the Church as Saint Helena, was secretly a Christian. His father, if not a baptized Christian, was sympathetic toward the Church.[11] The evidence of his inclinations was that as a general during the persecution he ignored orders to kill Christians and only allowed property destruction in the areas under his control. Thus Constantine knew the faith, was probably raised in the faith, and was at least favorable to the Church, if not a believer in secret. After the death of his father, Constantine led his father's loyal legions in a march on Rome in order to liberate the city from the tyrant Maxentius. In a famous story (of which there are several versions), Constantine had a divinely inspired vision just prior to the decisive battle in the year 312.

According to the story, Constantine was camped outside the city of Rome, near the place where the Milvian Bridge had been. Maxentius had had the bridge destroyed to prevent Constantine from entering the city. While praying, Constantine looked up into the sky and saw a sign. Depending on the version of the story one reads, the sign was either a cross or a "monogram" of Christ.[12] He also saw (or heard) words something to the effect of: *You will conquer by this (sign)*. The symbol was placed on the shields and/or the standards of the legions, and (eventually) on Constantine's helmet. Regardless of the details of the story, Constantine proclaimed himself a Christian, went into battle under the banner of Christ, and won. This victory at the Battle of the Milvian Bridge established him as ruler over the western half of the Roman Empire.[13] The grateful citizens of Rome would proclaim Constantine "Liberator of the City, Founder of Peace."[14]

Within a little more than a decade, Constantine had defeated his other rivals to become the sole emperor of the Roman Empire. He believed that he owed his reign to God, not to his military expertise, his status in society, his wealth, or his family of origin; he certainly didn't entertain any claim to his own divinity. He saw himself as a new David, having conquered his Goliath(s) by the will of God, and apart from the will of God he would not have come to power. Like other ancient rulers, he believed that he won his battles because his God was greater than the gods of his enemies. But unlike them, he did not claim to rule by divine *right;* his leadership came by a *grant* from God that entailed serious obligations. Constantine recognized that with great power comes great responsibility and accountability, meaning that he was not above the law, and God could take away his power at any time. He knew he was not the highest authority; he answered to a higher power. His emperorship was an office of stewardship—taking care of the empire for the real King: God.

This is not to say that Constantine ruled as a Christian. He postponed his baptism until the end of his life, like many believing soldiers and government employees did at the time, to put off having to live up to the moral expectations of a baptized Christian. Nevertheless, it was during his reign that a Christian version of government began to come to light. For example, Constantine paid reparations to the Church, returning property taken during the persecutions, and paying for the building of the first basilica churches in Rome and elsewhere. He promoted the Christian emphasis on human dignity by discontinuing crucifixion as a form of execution and by discouraging the gladiator games. He also promoted the well-being of the laborer when he created the weekend (making Sunday a day of rest and religious observance).

But the most revolutionary thing Constantine did was to guarantee freedom of religion. Contrary to popular myth, Constantine did not create a union of church and state. As we noted earlier, religion had routinely been part of government, and participating in the state religion was mandated. The fact that during times of persecution, pagan worship was used as a pledge of allegiance proves that before Constantine, government and religion were united. But with the reign of Constantine, the empire was on the brink of something new—a separation of religion and government, in which each person worshipped according to his or her own conscience, according to his or her own free will.

Before the time of Constantine, no society in the world had ever had anything like religious freedom. Tertullian had complained on behalf of the Christians, "We alone are prevented from having a religion of our own."[15] But that wasn't entirely true. Christianity was not the only religion that was outlawed. Any cult that involved celebrations that were considered wild and indecorous was suppressed. Any cult that was suspected of practicing magic or human sacrifice (like the Druids) was outlawed. And any group that was seen as too new (like Christianity) was suspected of political motivations and was also outlawed. In short, any religion that was perceived as un-Roman could be a target for persecution. The cult of Isis, for example, was constantly under attack by the Roman authorities, and the emperor Tiberius once used a local scandal as an excuse to destroy a temple of Isis and crucify its priests.[16] On more than one occasion, the Romans tried to desecrate the Jerusalem temple and massacred crowds of Jews whom they feared would become unruly.[17] And both Tiberius and Claudius tried to expel all the Jews from Rome.[18]

Roman religion, as we have seen, was not a matter of personal faith. Religion was a matter of patriotism, and to fail to participate in the state religion was to be a traitor. Roman leaders feared that the national gods would be offended if people didn't worship them, and they worried what the consequences might be. Many Roman government jobs included responsibilities to provide for, or even preside over, pagan sacrifices. But Christians, once they had converted, rejected the state religion, and it is easy to see why the Romans could not tolerate this. But Constantine separated patriotism from religion, not least by confessing his ultimate loyalty to a higher power—and one not connected to the traditions of Rome. Constantine separated government leadership from pagan cultic duties, so that government officials could be Christian. Despite the myth, Constantine never made Christianity the official religion of the empire, and he never forced anyone to convert to his faith. The truth is, Constantine was the one who issued the law that mandated religious tolerance in the Roman Empire.

In the year 313, Constantine sent an imperial letter to the Senate and the bishops, which we now know as the Edict of Milan. The letter was actually from both Constantine and his co-regent Licinius. This Licinius, a pagan, later turned against Constantine, and Constantine defeated him in the final struggle to become sole emperor over the whole empire. Even though the letter came from both Constantine and Licinius, the language and the way it refers to God show that Constantine himself was the originator of the edict. It states:

> *When we, Constantine and Licinius, emperors, had met at Milan, and conferred together with respect to the welfare and security of the empire, it seemed to us that, among those things that are profitable to humanity in general, the reverence paid to the Divinity merited our first and chief attention, and that it was proper that the Christians and all others should have liberty to follow that mode of religion which to each of them appeared best, so that God, who is seated in heaven, might be benevolent and favorable toward us, and to everyone under our government. And therefore we decided it would be a beneficial course of action, and one highly consistent with right reason, that no one should be denied the freedom to join himself to the rites of the Christians, or to whatever other religion his mind directed him. . . .*
>
> *. . . the open and free exercise of their respective religions is granted to all others, as well as to the Christians. For it is fitting for the well-ordered state and the tranquility of our times that each individual be allowed,*

according to his own choice, to worship the Divinity, and
we mean not to detract anything from the honor due to
any religion or its devotees.[19]

In issuing the Edict of Milan, Constantine did not outlaw
paganism, and he did not make Christianity the only legal religion in the empire. He legalized Christianity, giving Christians
freedom of worship. But he extended that freedom of worship
to all religions, no less than the freedom of religion clause in
the Bill of Rights of the United States. Furthermore, Constantine believed it would be wrong to turn the tables and persecute the pagans, even though it could be argued that they were
the former persecutors. Following the nonviolent precedent of
Christians suffering persecution, the answer to persecution
was not a reversal of the roles of persecutor and persecuted. He
forbade any retaliation, and he counseled Christians instead to
evangelize and invite pagans to convert. But notice the prominent free will language in the Edict of Milan, language that
affirms the rights and dignity of every individual, and the necessary freedom of the individual to act according to conscience.
Constantine believed that faith had to come by free will, and
that forcing belief was an exercise in futility.[20] Forced conversions would only dilute the membership of the Church and
compromise its integrity. People must be free—even free to be
wrong. In a letter to the eastern provinces, Constantine wrote:

Therefore, let those who still delight in error, be made
welcome to the same degree of peace and tranquility
which believers have. For it may be that this restoration

*of equal privileges to all will prevail to lead them into
the straight path.*[21]

Constantine said he wished to see the whole world converted, but his priorities were the unity and peace of the empire,
and to that end he offered freedom of worship to people of all
religions. And it was because of this that it was possible for
the Church to begin to influence the world on a greater scale,
and for the Christian vision of government as stewardship to
begin to take root through his reign—by the grace of God, and
even in spite of his failings as a self-proclaimed believer. And
that Christian ideal of government would take root to such an
extent that now, even though the ideal is hardly ever realized,
we know what we are striving for. Many Christians in the
early Church saw the rise of Constantine and the legalization
of Christianity as the beginning of the so-called millennium,
in which Christ reigns on earth, influencing the world through
the Church (Revelation 20:1–3).[22]

Unfortunately, Constantine's vision of unity and peace
through religious freedom was short-lived. After his death,
the empire was torn by the rivalries (and heresies) of his sons.
Eventually, a cousin came to the throne, a lone and bitter sur-
vivor of a series of attempts to murder all the relatives who
might claim the right to rule. His name was Julian, and he is
known to history as "Julian the Apostate." Not only was Julian
a pagan; he was an old-school anti-Christian, and his primary
agenda as emperor seems to have been the eradication of the
Church. But rather than engage in direct persecution (though
he turned a blind eye when provincial governors persecuted

Christians), Julian tried to squeeze the Christians out of prominent positions in society. For example, he made it illegal for
Christians to teach in the Roman schools, and he intervened in
ecclesiastical disputes in ways that diminished the authority of
certain bishops. Still, despite his attempt to rid the empire of
Christianity, he recognized that the Christians were the ones
taking care of the poor and the sick—even the pagan poor and
sick—and he admitted that this was an embarrassment to the
traditional pagan culture. He tried to create a social welfare
system without the foundation of Christian morality, but this
effort failed because he could not get wealthy pagans to step up
enough to provide care for those they saw as "beneath" them.

Julian's attempt to imitate the social outreach of the Church
is indicative of other pagan imitations of Christianity. Some
of the Roman cults also imitated elements of Christian liturgy.[23] The popular myth that Christian holidays were taken
from pagan holidays is actually the opposite of the truth—
the pagans co-opted the Christian holidays.[24] In the midst of
Julian's attempts to bring back the religious intolerance of
Roman culture, even the pagans acknowledged that the Christian Church had grown because it offered benefits to humanity,
and the Roman state could not replicate that success because
it lacked the Christian morality that gave rise to the ethic of
social responsibility. When a Christian emperor was again on
the throne, his reaction to his predecessor's attempt to reinstate
religious intolerance was a "never again" attitude.

The emperor Theodosius I (r. 379–395) made Christianity
the official religion (and the only legal religion) of the Roman
Empire in the year 380, through the issuing of the Edict of Thes-

salonica. The official religion of the Roman Empire became the faith of the apostles and of the bishops—specifically, the faith as defined by the Council of Nicaea and its creed.[25] The following year, Theodosius convened the second ecumenical council in Constantinople, which expanded the creed to create what we know as the Nicene Creed.[26] Theodosius made pagan worship illegal and sanctioned the destruction of pagan temples (though it seems he did not enforce this order). In any case, Constantine's ideal of religious freedom was gone, and religion and government were once again united. When all the dust had settled, the state religion was Christianity, and although the government was not what we could call Christian per se, the Christian emperors made it possible for the Church to influence the world and infuse the cultures of the known world with Christian values.

By now it should be clear, and perhaps it should go without saying, that the ideas that no one is expendable, that all people are created equal, that every life is sacred, and that everyone should be free to follow his or her own conscience—these are not political ideas; they are *Christian* ideas. No culture had ever embodied these values before there was a Christian culture.

Is the United States the New Rome?

So what about the United States? Is the United States more like the pre-Constantinian Roman Empire, or more like the Christian ideal of government as stewardship?[27] Perhaps it's a little of both. In some ways, our government was patterned after the Roman Republic, but with more emphasis on the rights of everyone (actually only white male property owners at first) to have a voice in the decisions that affect us. But much of the time we are really a kind of aristocratic oligarchy, in which only the rich can afford to run for office, as they buy votes with promises of what their party will do for the voters. It seems that despite our best efforts, we humans tend to regress to a self-centered utilitarianism that ultimately favors the wealthy and/or protects the privilege of the powerful.

Writing in about the year 1770, Scottish law professor Alexander Fraser Tytler said:

> *A democracy cannot exist as a permanent form of government. It can only exist until the voters discover that they can vote themselves largesse from the public treasury. From that moment on, the majority always votes for the candidates promising the most benefits from the public treasury with the result that a democracy always collapses over lousy fiscal policy, always followed by a dictatorship. The average of the world's great civilizations before they decline has been 200 years. These nations have progressed in this sequence: from bondage to spiritual faith; from faith to great courage; from courage to liberty; from liberty to abundance; from abundance to selfishness; from selfishness to complacency; from complacency to apathy; from apathy to dependency; from dependency back again to bondage.*

We don't agree with this statement completely, but Tytler makes an interesting point, especially since the United States is now over two hundred years old, and we appear to be at the point of transitioning from abundance to selfishness. As we will propose in the concluding chapters, the way to prevent the decline that Tytler predicted is to make sure that we don't fall into complacency and apathy.

The good news is that there are many ways in which the United States is not like the Roman Empire. First, we eventually rejected slavery.[28] Christian values won out over the economics of power, which claimed the "right" of some people to own other human beings. Also the United States has not tried to expand our borders through colonization.[29] It could be argued that a primary reason for the fall of Rome was that it attempted to conquer and colonize beyond a tipping point, and that the empire grew too big to govern.[30] The size of the empire combined with the greed of the emperors who could not share rule and the exponentially increasing cost of defending the far-flung borders caused the empire to cave in on itself. Thankfully, the United Stated has not made this same mistake, perhaps because we began as a collection of colonies.

Finally, the United States was founded on the principle of religious faith and religious freedom. Both the U.S. Bill of Rights and the Edict of Milan were born out of religious persecution, and the leaders behind these documents desired peace among a people who would be given the freedom to believe as they chose. We often refer to this aspect of our government as a separation of church and state, but the truth is that the founders of the United States never intended to create a state without religion. They assumed that the government would be run on Christian principles.[31] It is a myth that the founders of our government were Deists. Every one of the signers of the U.S. Constitution was a Christian, with the exception of Benjamin Franklin, who was the only true Deist. It had become fashionable in that day to use the language of Deism (speaking of God in nonspecific terms as a generic higher power)—this was the politically correct lingo of the day—and therefore many Christians spoke and wrote like Deists in the interest of tolerance and religious freedom, though their personal beliefs were specifically Christian.[32] At its best, the government of the United States is based on the Christian principles of the equality of all people, and the right of all people to believe and worship as they choose. Furthermore, it is not a good society that creates good people, as Plato claimed; individuals being good is what creates a good society. And when it comes to rulers, the powerful have a responsibility to serve and protect the powerless.

Where we go wrong in our country is when we forget that patriotism is not the same thing as faith, and we fall into the trap of imitating the pagan Romans when we make a particular faith, even Christianity, a litmus test for loyalty to the country. We must avoid this, because it always leads to intolerance, restriction of freedom, and a loss of peace. Ironically, the overzealous connection of Christianity with American culture and patriotism only pushes anti-Christian elements to go to the other extreme. We are now seeing the rise of organizations that oppose all religion, as if to argue that our society should be stripped of its Judeo-Christian foundation. What we need is not one extreme or the other: not the establishment of an officially Christian state, nor the sterilization of government so that it is devoid of faith. We need for people to have the freedom to worship according to their conscience, in a state that is based on the assumptions that God is love, and that we are expected to love our neighbors.

The separation of church and state is meant to keep the government out of the business of religion (to prevent the government from establishing an official religion), not to keep religion out of the government. The Establishment Clause and the Free Exercise Clause of the First Amendment were meant to ensure the freedom of religion, not curtail it.[33] Yet all too often we find the concept of separation of church and state used as a means to inhibit the practice of faith—a topic we will return to in the final chapters. For now it is enough to say that in the post-Christian secular world (which looks a lot like the pre-Christian pagan world) it would not be surprising for Christians to find themselves faced once again with the choice between empire and kingdom, between Caesar and Christ.

Conclusions and Consequences

The Church offers the world an alternative to empire. We call it the kingdom of God, but we're not simply talking about that future aspect of the kingdom, when Jesus returns.[34] We're talking about the ways in which the values of the kingdom are to be lived in the world, as in the Our Father when we pray, "Thy will be done on earth as it is in heaven." And although God's will is not always done in the here and now, Christianity has provided the foundation for the best expressions of human government. Specifically, in our Western version of democracy, all of our ideas about the equality of people, the value and dignity of every human being, and the right of every individual to be free to exercise his or her own free will and have a stake in his or her future—all of these are Christian concepts, a gift of the Church, as revealed by God. Religious tolerance is a Christian idea. Even the separation of religion and government is a Christian idea, but underpinning it is the assumption that the government is both founded on the ethics of loving one's neighbor and prevented from restricting religious freedom. Thus freedom even extends to an individual's right to reject God, as long as that person lives peacefully.

Leadership, for the Christian, is a theological concept, based on some of the same principles that were evident in the controversy over Pelagius. The Church rightly concluded that where there is good work done in the world, it is not from God alone, nor is it the work of people apart from God. It is the result of a cooperation between God's grace and people responding to it. Therefore, in government, leaders are meant to be in a partnership with God, to do God's work in the world and carry out God's priorities of serving those whom they rule, and also protecting the vulnerable. Leadership is therefore a form of stewardship, in which leaders are responsible for God's people and resources (including environmental resources). On another level, that cooperation between God and rulers should be mirrored in a partnership between the rulers and the ruled, so that those who are not in power are able to have a voice and truly influence those who are in power. In other words, government should serve the people, not the leaders.

The controversy over the Donatists can also inform our

understanding of government. Remember that the Church concluded that it must be inclusive, that Christians cannot presume to "weed out" those whom some might consider impure
or unworthy, and that unity was a priority. In a nation, as in
the Church, diversity is a strength, and this notion has implications for policies on immigration. Any country must be very
careful that in closing its borders to immigration it is not contributing to its own demise. The population of the United
States would be in decline if not for immigration.[35] The theological principle at work here is that for the Christian, everyone is the neighbor whom we should love (Luke 10:29–37), and
everyone is a child of God, regardless of status or origin. All
are created equal, no one is expendable, and no one should be
excluded from the benefits of society.

Finally, Christian morality demands that governments protect those who cannot protect themselves, including children,
infants, and the pre-born. The Church, when it is at its best,
rejects violence as a political tool and questions the validity of
capital punishment. And as we have seen, the failed agenda of
Julian the Apostate demonstrated that there is no public welfare without Christian values, and any government worth preserving must be willing to acknowledge this fact, for the good
of all its people, Christian and non-Christian alike.

In the revolution of the state the Church transformed the
world's understanding of government. Most people today
would agree that the best governments are those that defend
human rights—those in which the strong protect the weak.
The Christian Church, first by criticizing Roman culture, and
then by converting it, instilled a new set of values, replacing

the idea that some people are expendable with the idea that everyone is valuable. Thus, religious freedom is about more than the freedom to worship according to one's conscience—it is also about freedom from persecution, oppression, and exploitation by one's own government. It is freedom from a class system that assumes that some are born to rule and others are born only to be ruled over. And religious freedom is freedom from fear—a freedom that can only come from living in a society in which the leaders are considered stewards of their people and resources.

CHAPTER 9

THE CHURCH CAN CHANGE
THE WORLD AGAIN

Have you ever heard someone say that if Jesus returned today, he wouldn't recognize the Church? This sentiment seems to pop up now and then, often on social media, posted by people who revel in finding fault with the Church. It's true that in every age of history, Christians have done things that would make Jesus cringe. But to say that he would not recognize the Church is to imply that somewhere along the way the Church went completely off track—that the Church that Jesus founded was meant to be something other than what it is. The truth is, Jesus promised that this would never happen. As recorded in Matthew 16:18, Jesus said to his apostles, "On this rock I will build my Church, and the gates of the netherworld will not prevail against it." This is Jesus's promise that the Church will never go so far astray that it becomes something that it was not meant to be. If it did—if it ever became something Jesus would not recognize—then hell will have won.

But that cannot happen. Not because the Church is perfect, but because our Lord is perfectly faithful in keeping his promises. There will always be times when Christians fail to live up to the standards set by Jesus and the apostles. There certainly have been times when the Church as an institution has failed to embody its own values. But those values survive the failures, and the foundation of the Church (including its creeds and sacraments) is not shaken. So we are confident that if Jesus returned today, he *would* recognize the Church. He would recognize the Church in its doctrines, in its worship, and in its service in the world. And he would also recognize the world, because our world is looking increasingly like the world of the Roman Empire in which Jesus lived and ministered.

The title of this book is *Seven Revolutions: How Christianity Changed the World and Can Change It Again.* In the previous chapters we have described seven ways in which the Church changed the world for the better, by emphasizing, for instance, human rights, love of neighbor, freedom, and stewardship. But our point is not simply to raise awareness of the contributions of the Church. We believe that the Church can change the world for the better again. So if the Church can change the world again, how will that happen? For us to answer that question, we have to be clear that the Church, as we are talking about it, is not simply an institution. It is not as though we can sit back and wait for bishops and other clergy to change the world. Instead, when we think of the Church, we have to be mentally looking in the mirror. We are the Church. You are the Church. So, whatever the Church is going to do, it can do it only if you step up and participate in it. This is the New Evangelization.

The good news is that the Church is universal—it exists throughout the world. So we are not talking about any one denomination or branch of Christianity. We are talking about worldwide Christianity: Catholic, Protestant, Orthodox, Coptic, and all the rest. You are part of something much bigger than yourself, but at the same time you are not insignificant because the universal Church (and the world) is counting on you to make a difference wherever you are.

On one hand, you can be encouraged by the fact that most of what is good in the world, in terms of human rights and improved quality of life for all people, is a product of the presence of Christianity in the world. The Church has changed the world for the better over the course of history, and it continues to do so. On the other hand, we are recognizing something that has been going on for a while now: in many places the influence of the Church on the world is diminishing. In Western cultures, even where the majority of the people claim to be Christian, many countries have long been experiencing a decline in the practice of Christianity (most often measured by church attendance), and we are now even seeing the creation of laws that restrict the public practice of religion, reducing freedom of religion to the freedom of private belief.[1] In other cultures, the situation is even worse, with overt government-sanctioned persecution. Religious persecution is on the rise in the world, and especially in those countries where it is written into law, persecution shows no signs of decline.

In truth, there are many kinds of religious persecution, some more subtle than others. And in many places, including our own United States, Christians are increasingly faced with the choice of either conforming to secular culture or being marginalized by a society whose values are now driven by the "principalities and powers" of political, academic, and media elites. Because of the Church's diminishing influence on culture, we are now living in what many have called a "post-Christian" world, and as we have noted, post-Christian secularism looks a lot like pre-Christian paganism. What is more, the most disturbing similarity is that both pre-Christian and post-Christian cultures tend to be anti-Christian.

The Church Changed the World for the Better

As we have shown, Christians and Christianity have made the world a better place. The seven revolutions of the Church can be broadly grouped into two categories: the protection of all human life, and the protection of each person's dignity and freedom. These improvements are based on the conviction that every human is a rational creature made by a loving Creator in his image.

Regarding the protection of all human life, the Church affirmed that since we are all made in the image of God, no one is expendable, and no one can be used or exploited by another as if they were property or a commodity. The Church rejected the common social hierarchies of the ancient world and affirmed that all people are equal, and equally valuable, in the eyes of God (Galatians 3:26–29).

Perhaps the high rate of infant and maternal mortality in ancient Rome contributed to a general desensitization to death, and in particular to the idea that women and children were less valuable to society than men. Maybe that's why every other

culture in the ancient world (with the exception of Jesus's Hebrew people) failed to see the value of all human life. All of the
other cultures assumed that some people are expendable. But
(the historical failures of some Christians to fight for human life
notwithstanding) the Church rejected such an idea, and, in the
big picture, Christians refused to accept the myth that great suffering and a desensitization to death had to be a part of life.

In a world where men were criticized for mourning the
death of a baby, where women and children were not protected
by the law, and marriage was a contract meant to facilitate the
consolidation of wealth, Christians affirmed the sanctity and
worth of every individual person—especially the most vulnerable. Women and children were not to be exploited, and they
certainly were not to be treated as disposable. Instead they were
to be protected and educated. The weak and the sick were to be
cared for, not abandoned. Violence was rejected. And the family
was empowered to be a place of safety for all members. Thus the
Church worked, and fought, for life—and eventually, Christians
converted the empire to their way of thinking. The legacy of the
Church, in the Western world especially, is a shared assumption
that civilized people must be concerned for human rights.

In the second category, the protection of each person's dignity and freedom, the Church went beyond basic human rights
and affirmed the freedom of every person to *define* his or her
own life. Foremost was the freedom for each person to worship
according to his or her conscience. The emperor Constantine,
in spite of his flaws and failings, understood that conversion
had to be voluntary, according to one's own free will. We also
have Constantine to thank for making Sundays a day off from

work—one day a week dedicated to religious observance. In this way, he facilitated the Church's understanding of the dignity of the laborer, who required a balanced life of work, rest, and prayer. Freedom of worship also means that a person has to have the free time to worship, and must be free from being worked to death. Laborers must not be exploited and deprived of peace, relaxation, and time with family.

Equally important is the Christian understanding of the afterlife as resurrection, as opposed to the philosophical afterlife of a disembodied spirit, or the pagan afterlife of a shadowy numbness (not to mention some people's belief that death simply meant annihilation and nonexistence). Christianity not only overcame death; it overcame the *fear* of death, giving people the freedom to live for others, and according to God's revealed will, without so much fear of self-preservation.

It would not be an exaggeration to say that we have the Church to thank for most of the best art that has ever been produced. This includes a wide range of music that simply would not exist without the influence of the Church. The Church also supported many of the world's most important scientific discoveries and inventions, and many Christians are directly responsible for advances in science and medicine. Thus humanity realizes its potential as created in the image of God only when people have the freedom to imitate their Creator by being creative.

The Church has been the patron of freedom, and one might even say the freedom to pursue happiness. This is not a selfish freedom, in which a few people have absolute freedom to do anything they want at the expense of others. This is not a bought-and-paid-for freedom that is the privilege of an elite class who enjoy it while the majority have little or no freedoms. This is a freedom that includes responsibilities—the responsibility to protect others, especially those most vulnerable to exploitation. Those in power have the responsibility to protect the lives, the dignity, and the freedom of the rest. Leadership is meant to be a form of service. Leaders are not supposed to serve only themselves and their own social class, but they are supposed to be the servants of those whom they represent. Since God is love, we are called to emulate God by loving our neighbor, and there is no one who is not our neighbor.

Therefore, when we speak of traditional Christian values, this is what we mean. We mean the protection of human life, which includes support for marriage and the family (as opposed to the apparent conviction of many of our celebrities that marriage is optional); and we mean the protection of human dignity and freedom, which includes ensuring the safety of those most vulnerable to abuse, exploitation, and destitution. And these values, which were built over the centuries via divine revelation and historic Christian consensus, must not be marginalized. Freedom of religion is more than freedom of worship. It is also the freedom of religious expression—the freedom to speak and live the faith.

Of course there have been times when Christians have gotten it wrong, and we have to acknowledge their mistakes; otherwise we run the risk that these mistakes will find new ways to pop up again. To the credit of Constantine and the bishops of the early Church, they did not turn the tables as soon as the persecution was over. They did not persecute the former persecutors. They knew that persecution (let alone revenge) is not an effective tool of evangelism, and they wanted to convert the world. But within the Church, the bigger threat in the fourth century was heresy, and there were times when Constantine and some of the bishops gave in to the temptation to discriminate against separatist groups on the fringes of the Church. And then in later centuries there were the forced conversions of Charlemagne, the catastrophe of the Fourth Crusade, the corruption of some medieval and renaissance popes and bishops, and the excesses of the Spanish Inquisition. Tragedies like these are examples of what can happen when the Church as an institution becomes too closely aligned with the current reigning political empire. More recently, of course, are the scandals surrounding the abuse of children by people in positions of leadership (not only in the Roman Catholic Church), and the failure of some leaders to deal adequately with those who were guilty.

Many of these scandals are well known, but it's important to point out that they are well known for two reasons. First, they are the exception to the rule. The vast majority of the history of the Church is characterized by good news that doesn't make headlines, because it changes the world slowly through the quiet faithfulness of individuals. Second, they are the popular excuses repeatedly trotted out as the reason to throw the baby Jesus out with the baptismal water. In other words, people use these embarrassing episodes in the Church's history as an excuse to reject the God whom we worship. The stated logic often goes something like this: "I wouldn't want to belong to any organization or worship a God that allows those things to happen." But God never sanctioned these abuses, and it's ironically both self-serving and self-defeating to reject God because of the failures of some of God's people.

The truth is that because accepting a relationship with God would mean making a commitment, or changing one's behavior, some people would rather focus on the Church's failures so that they have an excuse to dismiss the idea that they should belong. Not only is that a cop-out; it can be quite an effective tool in silencing the faithful. The faithful need to remind the Church's detractors that when they criticize the Church, they can only do so on the basis of standards of behavior that the Church gave to the world. In other words, *we know those things are wrong only because of the influence of the Church.* Before Christianity came along, all of those terrible sins: religious oppression, abuse of power, greed, and sexual exploitation—they were all business as usual in the Greco-Roman world. So when Christians are guilty of these things, it is because they have forgotten that the Church itself gave humanity a higher standard. In part, this book is a call to return to that higher standard, to encourage all Christians to practice what we preach and concretely demonstrate the positive effects of our values in the world.

The World Is Changing Back

As we find ourselves in a post-Christian world, there exists a growing neo-paganism that rejects not only Christianity but also much of the good it has done in the world. The trend is to attempt to undo what Christianity has done. With regard to the protection of all human life, we are seeing society revert to the idea that some lives are expendable, even if only for the convenience of certain people. Human life is once again being valued on the basis of utility, or based on what contribution the person in question might make—balanced against the burden he or she will be on parents, relatives, or others who might have to be responsible for that person. The proof is the growing acceptance of assisted suicide, as well as that abortion has become a politically powerful billion-dollar industry. There are now over one million abortions performed annually in the United States, with the total abortions since legalization approaching fifty million. That is more deaths by far than the number of U.S. casualties of all of our wars combined. Some estimate that as many as one-third of all babies conceived in the United States are aborted.[2] We are not blaming women who choose to have abortions, since that must be for many the most difficult decision they will ever face. We are critiquing a society that has abandoned the values that would empower it to support both of the victims of every abortion: the mother who feels she must make such a tragic decision, and her baby. A society that respected life would support motherhood, as well as adoption, which would make abortion unnecessary.

But perhaps it should come as no surprise that some people are now aborting their babies for no other reason than that the baby isn't the sex the parents wanted. There have been several high-profile cases in English-speaking countries outside the United States. An Australian doctor found himself in trouble with his medical board for refusing to refer a couple for an abortion when the only reason they wanted it was because their unborn baby was not a boy.[3] And the evidence suggests that in these cases, just as in the Roman Empire, more often than not it will be baby girls who are discarded.

With regard to the protection of human dignity and freedom, there is a growing effort to redefine the idea of what freedom of religion is; the end result is that atheism assumes a place of legitimacy demanding the rights of a religion, at the same time that the historic religions are dismissed as unworthy of our modern age. It is a strange double standard that says, "My beliefs (or lack of them) are as legitimate as yours, but yours are no longer acceptable." Perhaps this is nothing new, but it seems to have gained a new respectability among the intelligentsia of our society, in spite of the fact that atheists still represent such a small minority of the population. Many political, academic, and media elites have bent over backward to cater to this vocal minority, and in doing so have betrayed their own traditions. We have all heard of attempts to ban expressions of religious faith in public settings, some of which have succeeded.[4] Rather than calling for equal respect for all religions, a nonreligious minority is demanding that religion be removed from any visible place in our culture. Freedom *of* religion is now being defined as freedom *from* religion.

This new definition of religious freedom demands freedom from having to see evidence of someone else's religion. Rather than affirming religious freedom as the freedom to practice the religion of one's choice—not only out of sight in a designated holy place once a week, but in everyday life—an increasingly vocal segment is pretending that religious freedom should mean that those who hate religion should be free from having to be confronted with it. The result—and this is already happening in some places—is that sharing the Christian faith, or even talking about traditional Christian beliefs and values, can be outlawed as a form of blasphemy, discrimination, or even "hate speech." For example, there have been several cases in recent years of Canadian clergy accused of hate crimes when they voiced their views on religion and society. Fortunately, so far freedom of speech has won the day, but the trend continues. In the United Kingdom, Christians who evangelize in Muslim neighborhoods are accused of hate crimes. Recently, a United States Army presentation to active and reserve duty troops announced that a particular evangelical Christian ministry should be considered "a domestic hate group," and that soldiers could be disciplined for involvement in that group.

It is important at this point to clarify that our purpose is not simply to join in on the fist shaking, railing against this or that group or political position. We are not looking for a scapegoat, as if to say "those people" are the problem. The truth is, human nature is the problem. Because of original sin, we are given to temptation, and our default is always to fall back into selfishness. People tend to want to think of freedom in the Roman aristocratic sense of absolute freedom for themselves, and they are fearful of anything that seems to threaten that kind of freedom. This means that since society is made up of imperfect humans, there is a very real kind of social entropy, a "devolution" if you will, that makes the human race tend toward a regression to its baser instincts. Without the influence of the Church, humanity will always degenerate into the corruption of anti-life and anti-freedom.[5] Or we could broaden that statement to say that without the influence of a religion of love (God is love, so love your neighbor), people will be greedy for power over one another, and those who get the power will always turn back to treating those without the power as property to be exploited, or as expendable.

The Church Can Change the World Again

Just as we are tired of hearing people say that Jesus would not recognize the Church, we are also tired of hearing people talk about "re-imagining" the Church, as if the Church needs to be re-imagined for a new generation. We didn't imagine the Church in the first place, so we don't need to re-imagine it (nor is it our place to do so). The Church was founded by Jesus Christ and his apostles, and we want to affirm that Christ's vision for the Church is still alive, in spite of human failures throughout its history. The problem is not that the Church needs to change to conform to a new generation (Romans 12:2); the Church needs to reclaim its power to change the world.

Back when the Church was persecuted by the Roman Empire, there was no question that the Church was countercultural. The Church converted the (known) world and influenced it for the better. This was a mixed blessing, because subsequently the line between the Church and the world was blurred. That line is being drawn again, sometimes by the Church and sometimes by the world, and Christians today must realize that living the faith means being countercultural.

We are not saying that culture is inherently evil, or that all expressions of culture are sinful. The best of culture (even popular culture such as entertainment media) can be uplifting and encouraging of Christian values. But where culture is counter-Christian, Christians must be countercultural. The only alternative is to conform to the culture, and unfortunately every day we can see examples of Christians doing just that. Although polls suggest that a majority of people in our country still identify themselves as Christian, it is an unwitting collaboration of the nonreligious minority and the nonpracticing Christians that now drives the factors that influence our culture. These factors include politics, entertainment media, and consumer marketing.

Thus, in spite of the fact that the majority of people in many First World countries are self-identifying as Christian, they have let the minority define what is culturally acceptable. And many of those self-proclaimed Christians have jumped on the bandwagon along with the nonreligious and are working to discredit and abandon the historic values of their faith. Perhaps some will find their way to reading this book, or will encounter dialogue with someone who has read this book, and then perhaps they will become open to a more positive direction.

Maybe you've also heard that the Church is no longer relevant to the current generation. This is ridiculous. First of all, the mission of the Church is not relevance. Second, the definition of what is relevant changes by the moment and depending on the person, and the focus on relevance is in many ways a symptom of the very relativism that is part of the problem. Having said that, even if the Church is perceived as being out of touch with the current generation, the problem is with the generation, not with the Church.[6] Was Jesus being irrelevant when he called his own generation adulterous and sinful? (Matthew 11:16–17; 12:39–45; 16:4; 17:17; Mark 8:12, 38; 9:19; Luke 9:41; 11:29–32). Jesus shows us that part of the Church's mission is to call each generation back to the Christian definition of relevance—which means the affirmation of life, in reverence to life's Creator.

Therefore, changing the world again means reversing the social entropy and reaffirming the seven revolutions of the Church. It may also mean starting some new revolutions, or at least solving some new problems, but in general that will still mean convincing the world to realize the value of every human life and the dignity of every human person. The Church can overcome neo-paganism the same way it overcame the original paganism—by following the lead of the early Christians. But they were persecuted, and if we put ourselves out there to work against the trends in society, we will be opening ourselves up to persecution as well.

Or we could always just do nothing. During the time of the early Church, there was a wide range of responses to the dominant culture. We are not claiming that every early Christian was perfect or participated fully in promoting the Church's ideals. Some made great concessions to the culture in order to fit in and not make waves. At crucial times, when the Romans demanded pagan sacrifice as a test of loyalty, many Christians simply made the sacrifices to save their lives, or their livelihoods. And in the neo-pagan culture of post-Christendom there will be new forms of persecution, and with that will come new ways of giving in to the culture. Christians will be increasingly threatened with marginalization (as they are already), and even legal action, and will be tempted to compromise their beliefs for the sake of their livelihoods. More Christians will be called insensitive, or even hateful, for expressing their beliefs and sharing their faith. More Christian business owners will face lawsuits for trying to run their businesses according to their principles. More restrictions on religious practice and religious expression will be written into law. This is not meant to sound like a doomsday message or some apocalyptic warning, but after all it was a persecuted Church that originally changed the world, and it will likely be a persecuted Church that will change the world again, bringing back the protection of the innocent and freedom of religion. The early Christians changed the world precisely because so many of them were willing to be removed from it rather than conform to it. Their peaceful resistance was their faithful witness to the gospel of love, and that is what converted their neighbors, their communities, and their world.

We understand that it's tempting to retreat. Many people feel immobilized by the criticisms of the anti-Christian minority, and the constant barrage of their reminders of past Christian failures. We understand that it's difficult to oppose injustice and to live sacrificially. It's tempting to hide away in private devotion, or, for some, to give up on the Church altogether. But to do that is to contribute to the social entropy that is hastening the decay of our culture. Remember that we participate in injustice when we do nothing to stop it. And the culture that winks at reality TV, brutal blood sports, and pornography is also the culture that turns a blind eye to domestic abuse, human trafficking, and genocide. Therefore, with this book we are calling all self-proclaimed Christians—even those on the proverbial fence.

We are calling them back to the core values of the faith, and to the practice of historic Christian values.

Just like the early Christians, we may find ourselves facing a choice between two kinds of sacrifice. We will either sacrifice our place of comfort within society to speak up for life and freedom, or we will sacrifice our convictions and accept the current definition of freedom (that is, absolute freedom of convenience for the individual, and freedom from having to be confronted with expressions of religious faith that may convict one of selfishness). If we choose to speak and act against the trends of culture, we will need to support one another, just as the early Christians did. Remember that many people sacrifice their lifestyle completely by devoting themselves entirely to the service of the Church. Clergy and those in monastic communities give up family and physical love, ambition and ownership, and even a certain amount of their own personal freedom, in order to serve the world by serving the Church. Everyone is called to a different level of sacrifice, but no one is called to live without some kind of sacrifice. So we have to be intentional about what kind of sacrifices we are going to make. If we want to change the world, we have to be willing to put our lives, lifestyles, and livelihoods on the line.

As Saint Augustine realized, and wrote in *City of God,* one cannot be a citizen of both the human society and the kingdom of God. So for the Church to change the world, Christians will need to detach themselves from the world to a certain extent. To be in the world but not of the world, as the well known paraphrase of Jesus's teaching goes (John 15:19; 17:13–18). Just as surgeons cannot operate on themselves, Christians cannot change the world unless they remain to some extent distinct from it. On the other hand, we cannot give in to the temptation to be completely separate from the world. The Eastern monks were trying this until Saint Basil asked (as another famous paraphrase goes), *If you always live alone, whose feet will you wash?* In other words, we cannot love our neighbor if we have no neighbors (or if we don't know our neighbors). And Jesus warned against our limiting our contact with neighbors to only those who are like us (see the parable of the Good Samaritan, Luke 10:25–37). Even today, there are Christians who are isolationist, who separate themselves from their brothers and sisters in other Christian denominations.

The Church will not change the world again if Christians live as contemporary hermits, focusing only on the afterlife, or reducing the practice of the faith to something that happens internally, or only within the walls of the church building. We have to engage the culture if we want to convert it. Therefore the solution is a balance, not withdrawing from the world, but also not conforming to it. In the world but not of the world—distinct but not separate. We as the Church can be incarnated into the world to change it—but only if we engage it without letting it convert us.

Now if all this sounds like we are just singing another chorus of "Give Me that Old Time Religion," it's important to remember that we are working with a fundamentally different understanding of reality compared to the people who think that neo-paganism is a good thing, and that post-Christianity is a step in the right direction. Anyone who thinks that way has a completely different definition of truth. In fact, this definition is relatively new in the grand scheme of history, and it would have to be. According to this definition, truth evolves. As time goes on, people get smarter and more enlightened simply by virtue of the fact that they live later in time. Advances in science, medicine, and industry imply that modern philosophy is automatically more advanced as well (you can even see this assumption in the way the word *advanced* is used to mean "better"). Anyone who thinks this way assumes that they must necessarily have a clearer understanding of ultimate truths than those who lived in earlier times, and they would claim that they are certainly more enlightened than those who lived before the "enlightenment" of the modern age.

By contrast, historic Judeo-Christian faith is based on *revealed* truth. Ultimate truths cannot be discovered by the unaided human intellect. Truth comes from somewhere. It has a source, and that source is God, incarnate in Jesus Christ. Furthermore, truth does not evolve—it does not increase or improve with the passing of time—instead the situation is quite the opposite. Truth must be preserved and passed down from generation to generation or it will decay and fade from memory and eventually it will be replaced with speculation. This doesn't mean that every little tradition of the early Church must be preserved—we are talking here of ultimate truths. But religion is the very thing that preserves these ultimate truths down through the generations, and without this preservation (which takes place in the Church), truth will become corrupted. Eventually, what is true will be thought to be false, and what is false will be thought to be true—the truth of God exchanged for a lie (Romans 1:25)—because people have a great capacity to believe what they *want* to be true—that is, what is most comfortable for themselves. The apostle Paul spoke prophetically when he wrote (or dictated) these words:

> *I charge you in the presence of God and of Christ Jesus, who will judge the living and the dead, and by his appearing and by his kingly power: proclaim the word; be persistent whether it is convenient or inconvenient; convince, reprimand, encourage through all patience and teaching. For the time will come when people will not tolerate sound doctrine but, following their own desires and insatiable curiosity, will accumulate teachers and will stop listening to the truth and will be diverted to myths. But you, be self-possessed in all circumstances; put up with hardship; perform the work of an evangelist; fulfill your ministry (2 Timothy 4:1-5, NAB).*

"The time will come when people will not tolerate sound doctrine." It seems that time has come. Actually, it's probably true that this could be said of every generation since Paul's, human nature being what it is. But the point is that there are universal truths that do not change with the times. Some things are always true and some things are always false. Some things are always right and some things are always wrong. To protect human life is always right, and to subordinate the life of an unborn person to the lifestyle of another person is always wrong. To protect human dignity is always right, and to allow some people to be exploited for the material gain of others is always wrong. But those who are "diverted to myths" desperately want to believe that truth is relative and ever evolving, so that today's truths can conform to today's expediencies. They want to believe that people are more enlightened and that humanity is progressing toward utopia, so that they can ignore the reality of sin and pretend that they don't need to change or try to become better. This is a temptation for all of us. But Paul knew, as we do, that truth does not evolve. Truth has a source—Jesus Christ—and it is preserved and passed on by the Church. Even when leaders of the Church have failed to protect human life and dignity, the Church at large has nevertheless preserved these values and lived them in the practice of life and ministry.

Saint Athanasius, in his biography of the Egyptian ascetic Saint Anthony, wrote, "Where the sign of the cross is, magic is weak and witchcraft has no strength."[7] Throughout history, wherever and whenever the Church has been at its best, with individual Christians living its ideals in a spirit of humility and love for all their neighbors, in those places and times the Church has converted the culture around it. To paraphrase what Athanasius was saying, where the Church is strongest, evil is weakest.[8] We as Christians, when we work together as the Body of Christ, have the power to change the world. But as the Church concluded after the Pelagian controversy, we can't just sit back and wait for divine intervention to change the world. It's not all on God. But the good news is, it's not all on us either. When we act in the name of Christ, we are cooperating with God, participating in God's work in the world.

A Countercultural Church Again

Assuming we are committed to being the Church and changing the world again, we will have to go into this with our eyes open. There is already real persecution against Christians in many places in the world—in some places by governments dominated by other religions, in other places by the new paganism. But even where persecution is not literally life-threatening, there is a growing cultural persecution that threatens to marginalize Christians and cut us out of polite society. Based on the erroneous assumption that truth evolves, Christians who stand for the historic values of the Church are dismissed as backward, unenlightened, and superstitious. Those who hold traditional doctrines and live by traditional Christian ethics are criticized by society's elites as being behind the times and so not worthy of a place of respect in public discourse. The original pagans leveled the same charges at the Christians in the early centuries. Now the Church's influence in the culture is being eroded and erased. Entire books have been written about the fact that the last politically correct prejudice is anti-Catholicism. We would like to expand this to say that it seems like the last socially acceptable prejudice is hatred of "conservative" Christianity.

In an attempt to replace religion as an influence on culture, secularism has become a religion—and its creed includes intolerance of Christianity. Unfortunately, Christians are partly to blame for this when they capitulate to the pressure to conform to the latest trends of the culture, sometimes even to the point of seeming to apologize for being Christian. But what is possibly the greatest danger to the health of our society is that in the

United States, the religion of secularism is becoming the state religion—counter to the prohibition in our Constitution. And this phenomenon is not happening in the United States only but in other countries as well. Here are a few examples from our own context in the United States.

News media consistently refuse to refer to the pro-life movement as "pro-life," since that naturally sounds like a good thing. Instead, they break their own rule of allowing any group to define themselves, and they refer to the pro-life movement as "anti-abortion," or something similar.

Pro-life or other conservative organizations have been the victims of governmental discrimination when their applications for tax exempt status have been stalled or denied. Some organizations have been threatened with pressure from the IRS, or risk having their tax exempt status revoked over the question of whether they truly qualify as religious organizations. This brings up the bigger question of who gets to decide whether a group or organization is religious "enough" to qualify as a religious organization. In the new religion of secularism, the government will decide what constitutes a religion. We have already seen this kind of power degenerate into human rights violations in other countries. On a few occasions, the government has even tried to control how religious organizations choose their leaders, though thankfully so far the Supreme Court has upheld the right of religious organizations to choose their own leaders according to their identity.

Perhaps the most blatant recent example of secularism posing as a state religion was the attempt to enforce a health care mandate that would force religious organizations to financially support practices that are in opposition to their values. And although the unconstitutionality of this policy was recognized by the Supreme Court, its supporters have not given up. It is the great hypocrisy of secularism to criticize religion for "forcing its beliefs on others" when in fact this health care mandate would have done exactly that. And new laws are constantly being proposed that would override the Christian values of respect for life in favor of neo-pagan values that include the disposability of the most vulnerable.

Because of this trend toward pagan utilitarianism in the valuation of human life, Christian organizations find themselves in a very difficult position, which for some may mean deciding to close their doors. Some Christian social service agencies have already discontinued adoption services due to laws that would force them to compromise their beliefs. Other organizations, including small mom-and-pop businesses, face fines and even lawsuits if they insist on running their business according to their moral convictions. As a result, more and more Christian businesses could decide to close their doors—including schools and hospitals. It is a sad irony that some of the very ministries that were given to the world by the Church (such as schools and hospitals) are having to decide whether to compromise the integrity of their very identity or go out of business altogether. It will be interesting to see what kind of economic burden this places on the remaining institutions.

Assuming that we as the Church do not resign ourselves to quietly letting the world be stripped of religious faith, we will have to be ready to be strongly criticized when we speak up in support of our Christian values. Charges of discrimination and perhaps even legal action may occur when Christians fail to conform to the "new truths" of the neo-pagan world. This will be the new persecution, allowed and even applauded in places that supposedly enjoy freedom of religion (because they really mean freedom *from* religion). The things we have heard people say about Catholicism would be considered a hate crime if said against any other group, but, as we have noted, a prejudice against the Church is the last acceptable bigotry.

It is the great hypocrisy of secularism that traditional Christianity is dismissed as intolerant, and, in the name of tolerance, vehement intolerance toward Christianity is justified. Tolerance becomes hypocrisy when the collective mind of polite society decides that it is legitimate to marginalize the very tradition that created that society, and when that collective mind justifies this marginalization by calling the tradition intolerant.

But take heart, because Jesus himself said, "Blessed are you when they insult you and persecute you and utter every kind of evil against you falsely because of me" (Matthew 5:11, NAB). We could say that if you're not getting any criticism at all, it might be because you are hiding your light under a bushel (Matthew 5:13–16). Be careful of selling out to the culture—it's easy to do, and it is the more comfortable option. Beware of falling into the trap of believing that truth evolves and the new "truths" are more enlightened than the old ones. Values based on revealed truth, not human speculation, are what make the world a better place. And changing the world will require an integrity that recognizes, and embraces, the Church's role as countercultural.

So how do we as the Church, the Body of Christ, convert

the world again? How do we live in a world where we are dis-respected, and even seen as antisocial, and still change that world for the better? How do we do it without pointing fingers, blaming scapegoats, or creating an "us vs. them" animosity? We will conclude by offering some concrete suggestions in the final chapter.

CHAPTER 10

A CHRISTIAN'S TO-DO LIST FOR THE TWENTY-FIRST CENTURY

Do you remember the old song, "They Will Know We Are Christians by Our Love"? We hope that statement will always be true, but in the post-Christian world (as in the pre-Christian world), it will probably be the case that they will also know we are Christians by our countercultural approach to life, values, and morals. To put it another way, they will know we are Christians by what we *respect,* and by what we *reject.* They will know we are Christians by what we *reaffirm,* what we *resist,* and what we *refuse.* This is how we will work with God to change the world, and this is how the world will be converted again.

Now, does it make you a bad Christian if you can't do all of the things we are about to suggest? Of course not. The early Christians didn't do it all either. We're all called to different ministries and different levels of involvement. But like the early Church Fathers did, we submit our list of ideals as a call to action, to give you a handle on some concrete things you can do to get involved in changing the world (again).

Before we get to the specifics, it should go without saying that the first order of business is prayer. Speak to God and *listen* to God. Ask God how he wants you to become involved in changing the world. Read the Sacred Scriptures, and especially become more familiar with the New Testament. And don't skip out on going to church, where the people who support you gather, and where you receive grace and instruction (Hebrews 10:25).

Reject Isolationism

We begin with a reminder to resist the temptation to isolate yourself from "the secular world" (as if there is any part of the world that does not belong to God). We understand that it's easy to become discouraged by all the ways that society seems to be undoing the good that the Church has done, especially in the realm of respect for life. In the midst of what has been called a "culture of death," it's tempting to "circle the wagons" and limit your association to those with whom you agree. Admittedly, there were times when the early Christians did this, though that often occurred in the most dangerous times of persecution, and for the purpose of safety. But the mission of the Gospel is not self-preservation, is it? The mission of the Gospel is to baptize and disciple the nations (Matthew 28:19).

Still, some people take the approach of certain fundamentalists and others who refuse to socialize with people outside their own group. They write off non-Christians as "heathen" and other Christians as apostate, and they refuse ecumenical prayer, dialogue, and shared service. Others take the approach of the hermits and lock themselves in behind a wall of pious devotionalism. They focus on the "personal" relationship with Jesus to the extent that it leaves no room for service in the world. But even more people—and this is the one that's harder to see—adopt that new kind of stoicism that enables them to go about their day-to-day routine, numb to the injustices around them. This is very much related to the way the ancient world (and the modern world) can desensitize people to humiliation, suffering and death, by turning humiliation, suffering, and death into entertainment. In all of these cases, the end result is a lack of involvement in the real world and a failure to reach out in love and justice.

So let's beware of expressions of faith that are all internal. Depending on one's personality, it may be attractive to close our eyes and get lost in prayer and adoration. And of course this is a good thing, as long as at some point we open our eyes again and get up off our knees and go out into the world to be Christ to the people we find there. We should add that we also have to beware of the opposite extreme: expressions of faith that are all external. For other personality types, it may be attractive to keep busy—even doing the Lord's work—and neglect attention to prayer and devotion. Some of the heresies of the early Church led people into one extreme or the other—and that's often what heresy is: going to an extreme in one aspect of the faith to the exclusion of something else. Remember the story of Martha and Mary (Luke 10:38–42). In our spiritual lives, we all need a balance of devotion and service, and "Mary has chosen the better part," because we have to seek the Lord before we can serve him.[1] But the reason that we cannot be content with devotion alone is that it's selfish. It's a very individualistic expression of the faith, and our motivation seems to be to try to save ourselves only; we are not concerned with others.

One aspect of isolationism that people often don't recognize is the tendency to apply a consumer mentality to the choice of where a person worships. Many people "shop" for a church with the intention of finding one that meets their own needs, rather than joining the nearest church to their home, where they could participate in meeting the needs of the community. Many people travel great distances, passing several perfectly good churches along the way, to go to a "megachurch" every Sunday. We would like to take issue with that practice and suggest that instead Christians ought to be invested in their own community—attend the church in their neighborhood (parish)—and actually get to know their neighbors. Sure, you make some new friends when you attend a church in another community, but these commuter churches can become something more like a substitute for community—almost like a vaccine against community, giving you just enough of it so you don't get the real thing. If you aren't careful, the "small groups" of the megachurch can become another form of isolationism, a circle of comfort, protecting you from the world outside. Remember that the early Christians converted their pagan neighbors by knowing them, and serving them, and loving them. Evangelization works best when it happens within relationships.

Also let's beware of using technology as a substitute for community. A while back there was a television commercial in which a young woman voiced her embarrassment that her parents had very few social media "friends." Meanwhile, the parents were out doing things: riding bikes, going to dinner, all with real friends. The irony was obvious. The parents were living their lives, while the daughter sat in front of a computer screen in her apartment. It's too easy for social media to enable that stoic desensitization that encourages people to be numb to the suffering of others (or to think that clicking "like" is enough to support another person in their suffering). Let's examine our lives and think about whether we spend too much time on the computer, and whether we could spend some of that time out in the community or at our churches, volunteering to help others.

Isolationism can also operate on a national scale. In the United States there is an ongoing debate about immigration, and while this is not the place to enter into that debate in detail, Christians should remember that the early Church came to the conclusion that it is God's will for us to be inclusive. Not only our churches but also our communities and our country's borders must be open to the newcomer. It is not our job to pluck the weeds (Matthew 13); we shouldn't even be trying to figure out who the weeds are! We cannot close our doors—or our borders—to those who are different from us, provided, of course, that they intend to live according to the law of love for neighbor. Scientists tell us that, genetically speaking, diversity is strength. For example, purebred dogs are generally not as healthy as mutts. With people as well, we all know there's a problem with being "inbred." Just as it is with genetics, so it is with a community (and with a nation): diversity is strength. We must be open and ready to have as our neighbor, and as a fellow citizen, anyone who is willing to work hard and obey the law.

Isolationism is basically a form of individualism, which is itself a form of selfishness. It is a self-centered utilitarianism that evaluates things and people by their effect on "me." When people say that they have a right not to have their lives disrupted by an unplanned pregnancy, or when they say that they have a right not to be "offended" by public expressions of someone else's religion—in essence claiming the right to be comfortable and not to be inconvenienced—they are operating within a worldview that places themselves at the center. But this individualism also takes subtler forms, such as embracing the luxury of ignoring injustice simply because it is not happening in our own backyard, letting something like human trafficking go on as long as it doesn't affect us personally. We as Christians will need to resist this temptation in ourselves, and also to reject it in others, exposing the lie that it is an individual's right to preserve his or her comfort level even at the expense of others.

Therefore, REJECT isolationism in all its forms. RESIST simplistic and naïve forms of patriotism that closely associate Christianity with North American culture and assume that the United States (or your favorite political party) can do no wrong. REJECT foreign policies that ignore human rights violations in other countries, especially the oppression and persecution of Christians in other countries. REJECT immigration policies that make it difficult for law-abiding, hardworking people to share in the benefits of citizenship. REAFFIRM the openness and inclusiveness of the Gospel by petitioning legislators to make citizenship more accessible, and pressure your representatives to pass immigration reform. REAFFIRM that the American dream has always been a dream of immigrants and their descendants (and that if you live in the United States, most likely your ancestors were immigrants), and that diversity is one of the strengths of any country. Then get your congregation involved in supporting your undocumented neighbors and helping them get citizenship. Educate yourself and your congregation on the vital contributions that immigrants make and the ways that our current system places unnecessary hardships on them (check out the information on the website of the U.S. Conference of Catholic Bishops, www.USCCB.org). REJECT the consumerist approach to "church-shopping" and attend the church in your neighborhood. Get to know your neighbors and get involved in your community. REFUSE to spend too much time looking at a computer screen and approaching life through the tunnel vision of virtual community, and do something for someone else. Make your life's motivation not individualism or utilitarianism, but rather gratitude and compassion. This is the way you will contribute to making the world a better place. Finally, REJECT atheist claims of entitlement to make religion invisible in society. Get out there and be seen and heard!

Respect the Value of Every Human Life

The *Didache* is one of the earliest Christian documents (the earliest one we have that's not in the Bible), written around the same time as the Gospel of Matthew. In it, the author(s) includes standards for morality that are the expectations of any baptized member of the Christian community. One of the important values that the *Didache* covers is respect for all human life, including the pre-born. The belief that abortion is murder is not only a universal assumption in the early Church; it was part of the Christian's very identity—what distinguished Christians from the pagan world around them.[2]

There are two important theological reasons for this conviction. First, every person is created in the image of God (and that image is present from the moment of creation: conception). Second, the incarnation itself has implications for our understanding of when human life begins. The incarnation was when the divine and eternal Word of God became a human. But this "becoming flesh" (John 1:14) did not happen at Jesus's birth. The incarnation took place at the annunciation. In other words, The Word became flesh at Jesus's conception. Therefore, to deny the humanity of a pre-born baby means denying the humanity of Jesus in the womb of Mary. For this reason (and others) the Christian conviction has always been that abortion is simply another method of infanticide.

As we know, the Romans not only allowed abortion, they also allowed for the exposure (discarding) of newborns, if only the father decided he didn't want the baby. In a way, even the Romans recognized that there was no real difference between a fetus and an infant; they allowed the killing of both. Christians, on the other hand, didn't just oppose abortion and exposure; they went out and picked up the discarded babies. And that's what we need to do today. The Church will have to continue to lead the way in promoting adoption—not only as an alternative to abortion, but also as an alternative to expensive and complicated (and morally questionable) methods of artificial conception.

The Christian respect for life is not only applied to the beginning of life. Christians have always rejected any philosophy that places value on a person based on what he or she can contribute, or that devalues a person based on some measure of the burden that the person might present to others. Christians believe that those who are weaker should be protected (see 1 Corinthians 12). The family must be supported and strengthened so that children can be protected from exploitation. The vulnerable must be protected from human trafficking and the pornography industry. Anything that makes the human body a commodity is a form of slavery—and also a form of human sacrifice to the gods of commercialism—and therefore it must be resisted. When human flesh is valued for the ways in which it can be exploited, or when it is devalued and considered expendable, the Christian should be outraged.

In current times, there are movements to bring back Roman notions about what is acceptable at the end of life— suicide, euthanasia, and capital punishment. Before long even the Roman taste for public execution could return, and killing could become a strange combination of entertainment and catharsis. Being "pro-life" means more than just opposing abortion. It also means opposing the exploitation of women and children, brutal blood sports, euthanasia, assisted suicide, capital punishment, and closed borders.

There have been some encouraging signs of hope with regard to respect for life. Some states have written laws banning late-term abortions or requiring ultrasounds so that a mother can see her baby before making a decision about abortion. In other cases, states have implicitly acknowledged the humanity of a fetus by charging a man who caused a miscarriage with murder, or by charging a man who killed a pregnant woman with two counts of murder. We have seen a decrease in capital punishment (or at least an increase in delayed executions). And we have ongoing talks about immigration reform, and proposals for legislation. We have even seen a few encouraging Supreme Court decisions regarding the exercise of religious faith. The Church will need to build on these successes, encouraging the creation of laws that protect all human life, including life in the womb. Maybe you know that in the United States, people of African descent only became citizens protected by law when the government passed the Thirteenth and Fourteenth Amendments. We will need similar constitutional amendments to protect the rights of the most vulnerable.

Finally, it should go without saying that there is no room for racism in the Church. Since all people are created equal, and equally in the image of God, all must be treated as equally valuable, and no one should have their opportunities limited on the basis of their skin color or ethnicity. The problem is that there are subtle ways in which racism still exists, in the form of privileges that are not available to everyone. Those of us who are in the majority (that is, we are white) often don't see these inequalities precisely because we benefit from them. We need to become more aware of racism and point it out when we see it, so that steps can be taken to continue to eradicate it. Just as the Church was at the forefront of abolishing slavery and affirming racial equality, it must continue to be in the business of exposing and eradicating racism. The Church that rejected the Jew/Greek distinction (Galatians 3:26–28) must now continue to reject the injustices that come from distinctions of skin color and ethnic origin.

Therefore, REJECT the idea that any human life is expendable or disposable. REJECT the idea that anyone can place a value on human life based on potential contribution or burden. These ideas have so infected our culture that we even have an epidemic of disrespect among and between people. So RESIST the assumption that a person has to earn your respect and REFUSE to treat anyone with anything less than respect. RESIST racism, and speak up when you see it. REFUSE to participate in racial discrimination, even when it benefits you. REAFFIRM that all people are made in God's image by expanding your circle of friends to include people of other colors. It might not be easy, but do it anyway. REAFFIRM the family as a place of safety for men and women, and as the protector of the young. Support ministries that care for the victims of abuse and that work for the safety of women and children. REAFFIRM the option of adoption. RESIST the presence of abortion providers in your community. REAFFIRM the sanctity and dignity of all human life by donating, volunteering, protesting, and voting. Speak up for those who cannot speak for themselves. Be the power of the powerless by working on their behalf. Pressure legislators to defund and dismantle the billion-dollar abortion industry. Petition your representatives to create a constitutional amendment protecting the pre-born. Yet REFUSE to blame or demonize women who have had abortions, recognizing that they are also victims of the neo-pagan culture. REAFFIRM that every human is made in the image of God by working to eliminate human trafficking, assisted suicide, and capital punishment from our culture. Finally RESIST the temptation to use human flesh as entertainment through pornography or brutal combat sports.

Reject the Culture of Celebrity and Humiliation as Entertainment

The popularity of so-called reality television shows demonstrates that they have become the new Roman circus of the post-Christian age. The pagan spectacles of Rome have been reborn in the pagan spectacles of Hollywood. It is one thing to make an industry out of a gossip culture that pretends every detail of a celebrity's life is news, but now we even turn people without any real talent into celebrities, simply because they have chosen to sell their privacy.

We understand that it's tempting to try to escape from the boredom or drama of one's own life (or to try to find a way to feel better about it) by viewing the drama of someone else's life. But like the spectacles in the Roman arena, today's spectacles are idolatrous—and we even call some of these people idols! We are encouraged to follow every detail of their personal lives, as though their lives are worthy of our attention, and sometimes even to the neglect of our own lives. And although many of these celebrities would claim that they never wanted to be role models, they are emulated by people who now think it is acceptable to consider marriage both optional and recyclable.

But even if we think we can watch this kind of entertainment and separate our own lives from those of the downwardly spiral, we are not simply detached observers. Like the people who watched the spectacles and pagan rituals of ancient Rome, we participate by observing. Remember, the third-century priest Novatian wrote (and we're paraphrasing again): *What we are not allowed to do, we are not allowed to watch.* When we watch reality television or read gossip media, we support the very culture that turns a person into a commodity. This does not mean we can't enjoy fictional entertainment. There is nothing inherently wrong with movies and television shows, and sometimes laughter really is the best medicine. But when we support the kind of entertainment that exploits the real lives of real people, we become partners in that exploitation.

Recognizing the dignity of every human being means refusing to watch those people who have willingly sold themselves to the humiliation of reality television. It means refusing to participate in the gossip culture and it means rejecting the new spectacles that exploit people for commercial gain (even with their consent).

Therefore, REJECT the idea that there is a hierarchy of humanity in which celebrities are treated like royalty, but without privacy. REJECT the glorification of celebrities, especially when they don't respect the sanctity of marriage. REJECT the idea that indulgence leads to happiness, when in fact balance, discipline, and faithfulness lead to happiness. REJECT the message that sex can be recreational and without commitment. Hold out for marriage, and REAFFIRM that celibacy is the only appropriate alternative to the vocation of marriage. RESIST the temptation to watch or read media that turns the drama of someone else's life into entertainment. REFUSE to support the sponsors of reality television shows that invade people's privacy and showcase their humiliation. REAFFIRM their dignity, even when they are willing to sell it to you, by giving them their privacy and living your own life. REAFFIRM that art is the domain of our Creator, and go out and find some real beauty to appreciate. Experience nature, go hear some live music, or go to a museum—wherever you find true beauty, it's probably not on television. Better yet, create something beautiful yourself. Imitate your Creator by being creative.[3]

Respect the Humble, the Laborer, and the Poor

By rejecting the culture of celebrity, we are respecting the poor, because we are rejecting social hierarchies that place people on a scale based on their wealth, or lack of it. As we have seen, the Church has historically affirmed the equality of all people and rejected any social construct in which people are allowed to ignore the poor. The Church has also affirmed the dignity of work and rejected the assumption that people who have to work for a living are of a "lower class" than people who are independently wealthy.

As we have noted, the early Christians promoted the idea that those with money have a responsibility to share their resources with those who have less. The Christian message to the wealthy was as follows: The poor are to you what you are to God. In other words, just as you need God's compassion, the poor need your compassion (remember the parable of the Unmerciful Servant, Matthew 18:23–35). And in case *you* don't think of yourself as wealthy, keep in mind that in the big picture of the world's economy, if you're reading this book, it means you're probably very well off compared to most people in the world.

The *Didache* declared that no one should consider their possessions their own; people should consider everything they have as a gift from God—a gift meant to be shared. Everything we have has been entrusted to us by God, and it is meant to be used in the ministry of loving our neighbor. We are, in effect, the delivery system for God: he takes care of the poor through us. This is how we participate in God's work in the world and become a channel for God's grace.

But this means that we have to avoid assuming that the poor are poor through their own fault. That may be true for some, but we would do well to remember that all of us have made bad decisions at one time or another. It is not our place to judge the life situation of any other person, so we have to put such considerations out of our minds and only concern ourselves with the situation as it is. We deal with the need, and we give those in need the benefit of the doubt, saying, *There but for the grace of God go I.* The Church has always taught that giving to the poor is a form of penance, and also a form of evangelism. Throughout history people were converted because of the compassion of Christians. More can be converted by your compassion and by your generosity.

Therefore, REAFFIRM that giving to the poor is an act of faith in God's generosity. Give knowing that God's gifts keep on coming, and God will replace everything you give away (or if he doesn't, you didn't really need it). RESIST the temptation to wonder what the recipient will do with your gift. It only matters that you are generous, just as God has been generous to you. Of course, there's nothing wrong with giving in specific ways that are sure to put food in a hungry person's stomach— remember, the treasury of heaven is the stomach of the hungry. Give to the ministries of the Church, and give to Christian agencies that feed the hungry and care for the homeless. Give both globally and locally. Consider the early Christian practice of fasting and giving away the money you would have spent on the meals you skipped. Volunteer at a homeless shelter, food pantry, or soup kitchen. RESIST the exploitation of laborers (even those in other countries) who produce our food while being cheated out of a fair wage by the commodities markets. REAFFIRM the conviction of Saint Lawrence, that the poor and the humble are the treasures of the Church.

Reject the Creation of a Secular Religion of the State

As many governments in the world move toward various forms of socialism, history shows that they can also become prejudiced in favor of the kind of society that is religiously sterile. Many will openly claim that they are doing their people a favor by "liberating" them from religion. They perpetuate the lie that religion is always oppressive. As we have demonstrated in the preceding chapters of this book, Christianity has given the world freedom and human rights. Yet it is now supposed that governments can provide freedom and human rights without religious faith. We know this is a fallacy.[4]

No government can be allowed to force its religion of secularism on its people by making religious organizations pay for things they consider morally wrong, or indeed by presuming to decide which expressions of the ancient religions are religious enough to count as religions in the eyes of the state. Religious organizations must have the freedom to determine their own identity and choose their own leaders to remain consistent with that identity. Individuals must have the freedom to opt out of those elements of the culture that are contrary to their religious values. We cannot let any government come to the point of bundling conformity with loyalty, because that will only lead to a new version of persecution in which neo-paganism will become the litmus test of patriotism. The good news is, as history shows, even when there is persecution, the Church outlives every empire that tries to suppress it.

Therefore, REJECT the idea that truth evolves and people automatically get smarter over time, because that kind of thinking leads to the lie that atheism, or at least skepticism, is more enlightened than faith. REJECT the cultural relativism that says that anything goes except historical Christianity. RESIST the marginalization of Christians, especially in the realm of education. As the pagan emperor Julian tried to do in the fourth century when he restricted Christians from teaching in secular schools, Christian educators will be scoffed at, especially those who hold to traditional doctrines and values. Others will conform and call it progress. REFUSE that kind of conformity.

RESIST those who promote intolerance of Christianity in the name of tolerance. REAFFIRM the right of religious organizations to define themselves and their missions, and to choose their own leaders without interference from government. REAFFIRM the right of religious organizations to be free from having to support things they consider morally wrong. Support those religious schools and hospitals that RESIST governmental pressure to conform to a secular agenda. RESIST (nonviolently, of course) any government that drifts into a "separation of church and state" in which the Church is supposed to become invisible while some political ideology becomes the new object of faith and loyalty.

Respect Religious Freedom

The rejection of the secularization of culture and government goes hand in hand with the protection of religious freedom. In fact, they are two sides of the same coin. The very idea of freedom of religion was unheard of in the world before Christianity. Freedom was defined as license to do whatever one wanted, and it was a luxury of the aristocracy. Freedom was something that was bought, and you had to be extremely wealthy to be able to afford it. Freedom was all or nothing. The 1 percent had it all, and the rest had none. The 1 percent believed that their freedom gave them the right to exploit and abuse the other 99 percent. For the most part, people in ancient times were not free; they were bound under the authority of the royal or ruling class. The price of citizenship, indeed life itself, was absolute obedience to their "betters." Christian freedom, on the other hand, is real freedom without being absolute freedom (to exploit others). Leaders have a responsibility to care for the people. The people, in turn, are free to worship according to their own convictions.

As we began writing this book in 2013, we celebrated the seventeen hundredth anniversary of the Edict of Milan. Let's remember the ideal of respecting each person's free will and conscience. Let's stand up—and speak up—for religious freedom! That means that, while we must not be *of* the world, we still have to be *in* the world. Even though we as the Body of Christ remain distinct from the culture, we do not separate ourselves from it, because if we do we run the risk that it will shut us out and we will have no influence at all. We need more faithful Christian representation in politics, not so that American culture will be equated with Christianity, but so that there will be someone to critique American culture when it falls short of the Christian respect for life and freedom— for although it is true that the majority of representatives in Congress identify themselves as Christian, many do not vote according to the historic values of the Christian faith.

Therefore REAFFIRM freedom of religion by exercising freedom of speech. REJECT the criticism that Christian values are unenlightened, and demand that others respect your faith. REAFFIRM that the Church gave the world a great gift by clarifying monotheistic faith as trinitarian faith, and by redefining salvation and the afterlife based on the teachings of Jesus. RESIST attempts to dismiss the Church's historic doctrines as outdated or oppressive. REAFFIRM that creation is the result of a benevolent Creator, and as such human life and the earth are not meant to be disposable. Make the care of creation and the environment a priority. REJECT (by voting out of office) any leaders who do not see leadership as service, but who use their positions to serve themselves and the interests of their peers at the expense of the greater good. Get involved in politics, and work for the free expression of faith, and for the protection of the vulnerable. Petition politicians to put pressure on foreign governments that violate human rights and religious freedom by persecuting Christians—even when those governments are our allies.[5] Pray for your persecuted brothers and sisters around the world.[6] And REAFFIRM the claim of God on those whom he made in his image—that our loyalty is to our God first, and to our country second.

Reject a Defeatist Attitude

Remember the old maxim that it was improper to talk about religion in polite company? Now it seems it's perfectly acceptable to talk about the Church, as long as what's being said is negative. When this happens—when people bring out that tired litany of the Church's failures—the Christian's job is to speak up and defend the Church. And now that you have the information you need to tell the story of many of the good things Christianity has given the world, when you hear someone bashing the Church, don't hang your head and remain silent—stick up for your mother!

Don't let the naysayers get away with assuming that everyone agrees with them. And don't let the negativity seep into your mind. Keep the faith and keep fighting the good fight, with a strong commitment to prayer and almsgiving. Share your faith with your non-Christian friends and neighbors. Speak up! There is an often (mis)quoted saying, attributed to Saint Francis of Assisi. He is supposed to have said, *Preach the Gospel at all times; when necessary use words.* It may be that Francis never said this, but even if he did, the point was to emphasize the importance of living the faith and practicing what we preach; it was not meant to be an excuse to be silent. Certainly Francis would want you to speak up and share the faith, especially to defend the faith when others criticize it. Jesus said, "Your light must shine before others, that they may see your good deeds and glorify your heavenly Father" (Matthew 5:16, NAB). This means you cannot just do good works without letting people know *why* you do the good works. People have to know that we do what we do in the name of Christ, "so that they may see your good deeds *and glorify your heavenly Father.*" When you speak up for the faith, you will participate in the growth of the Church and the conversion of the world.

Therefore, RESIST the social pressure to suppress talk of Christ and the Church. REJECT the idea that Christianity is unenlightened; confront those who speak as though they think it is. Respond to editorials and social media posts that scoff at or mock the Church. Don't let them get away with assuming everyone out there agrees with them, and don't let them bully believers into silence. Write letters, write e-mails, and post comments. Show them we are here, and we're not going to shut up! REAFFIRM that it was Christianity that converted our world to the point where we assume the goodness of concepts like human rights and loving your neighbor—and then back up your words with actions that demonstrate how we practice what we preach. And when they respond by throwing the failures of Christians back at you, admit that we're not perfect, but remind them that Christ is perfect, and he's the one we follow and serve. Also remind them that we would not have any standards for critiquing human failures without the influence of the Church. In all cases, be charitable and generous. Resist the temptation to get angry or match their bitterness and hostility. Don't respond to hateful words with more hateful words. Respond with words of truth, but also words of love. Respond to persecution with generosity—both generosity of spirit, and generosity of resources. Surprise the world with joy and generosity!

Respect Your Neighbors

We conclude with what should be obvious: love your neighbor. But we understand how difficult that can be at times. Sometimes our neighbor can be perceived as the enemy. But just so there would be no excuses, Jesus also told us to love our enemies, and pray for them. It would be better if we didn't see anyone as our enemies, but that, too, can be difficult. We know what it means to feel so strongly about some of these issues that those who disagree with us can seem, at best, part of the problem, and at worst, downright evil. But even where there is real evil in the world, the people who perpetrate it are still people, made in the image of God. Our purpose here is to critique cultural trends and attitudes, not individuals, or even groups of people. Remember that the real enemy is bad philosophy, not "bad people." In other words, even though you may be strongly opposed to abortion, there is no room in the Church for violence (or even violent words) against those who provide abortions. It's a paradox, and it's not easy, but when Jesus told us to love our enemies, he didn't promise it would be easy.

And so we offer our love, respect, and service to our neighbors, no matter who they are—whether they are Christian or not—and even to our enemies. Remember that, if asked, everyone would probably say that they want to make the world a better place. Our disagreement is over what "better" means. Those who believe a better world means unrestricted access to abortion or restricting religious freedom—they are sincere; they are just misguided. Show them the light of love by responding to them with calm respect—even when they are hateful. Loving your neighbor even includes loving the one who ridicules you and the things you hold most dear. This is the only way to avoid the poisonous animosity that enables an "us versus them" attitude. That finger-pointing mentality is so easy. Our human nature wants someone to blame for the problems we see in the world. But the blame does not go to any one person or group of people—that would be scapegoating. The problem is sin itself, and we have to admit that we are part of the problem, too. We contribute to the very injustices we are talking about, sometimes by participating in them, and sometimes just by not

opposing them. Blaming and pointing fingers is counterproductive. Loving service while standing up for the truth is the
way to go here. Stay calm and be patient, because you have the
truth on your side.

Therefore, REAFFIRM that every person, even those with
whom you disagree, is worthy of your respect. Of course, you
are worthy of their respect too, and when they disrespect you, it
is your right to demand respect, for yourself and your Church.
But RESIST the temptation to demonize certain people, or to
try to lay the blame at the feet of any group of people. REJECT
hateful words or harsh speech—these only further polarize an
already divisive situation. REJECT violence. REJECT war as anything other than a last resort, and even then REJECT it when its
purpose is anything other than the protection of people and
their human rights. REAFFIRM that Jesus knew what he was
talking about then he said we should love our neighbors and
pray for our enemies. Do that—actually pray for those who
oppose you! Pray for those who threaten you or your way of
life. REAFFIRM that the religion of every faithful person is worthy of respect, as long as that religion promotes love of neighbor. But also REAFFIRM that Jesus called us to evangelize—to
share our faith with those who do not know him. Practice what
you preach. And finally, REJECT the argument that the Church
is part of the problem, and REAFFIRM that Christianity is actually the solution to the world's problems.

Now Get Started

We began by saying that this chapter is a call to action. But as you can see, it's a long and almost overwhelming list of suggestions. Now that you've finished the book, we would like to make one more suggestion. Go back through this last chapter, reading through the paragraphs of things to reaffirm or reject, and underline or highlight the ones that you feel most passionate about, or that you think you might be able to work on right away. Or perhaps underline some of the injustices that we often ignore on a daily basis, and think about what you might do to oppose them. When you're done, write out the list of things you underlined or highlighted and look it over. Pick one and get started. Find like-minded people and get involved in changing the world. If your church doesn't have a ministry that is specifically created to help the people you have in mind, or to stand up against that particular injustice, then start one! No one expects you to do everything on this list. Just pick one or two and take some action. Then later you may want to go back to the list and work on more of the suggestions. Some of them may be as simple as making a small change in your television watching habits. Others may require more sacrifice. Eventually, if you want to, you can go back to the chapter and add to the list. But whatever you do, don't reduce this book to a compilation of good information. Don't let it be something that just made you feel more strongly about what you already believed, or gave you a new insight. Take the information out into the world—allow this book to be the thing that helps you cooperate with God by participating in the work of the Church in converting culture. Embrace the fact that you are created in the image of God by imitating your Creator—be loving and creative in his name. Christianity changed the world, which means that *Christians* changed the world, and they did it by living their faith. Christianity can change the world again, but only if Christians continue to live their faith. The Church can convert the world again, but only when we remember that *we* are the Church.

Notes

Chapter 1

1. Adapted from *The Martyrdom of Polycarp*. Polycarp was martyred in the city of Smyrna (modern Izmir, Turkey) in about the year AD 156.
2. See James L. Papandrea, *The Wedding of the Lamb: A Historical Approach to the Book of Revelation* (Eugene, OR: Pickwick Publications, 2011), 20–26.
3. Rodney Stark, *Cities of God: The Real Story of How Christianity Became an Urban Movement and Conquered Rome* (New York: HarperOne, 2006), 92, 110. The cult of Isis had been outlawed in 58 BC, but was widely practiced in the later empire. The Romans' attempt at legislation against these cults was not always successful.
4. Tertullian, *Apology* 24. The third-century theologian Tertullian argued that although Christians did not participate in some aspects of society, they were good for the empire because of their morality and their prayers.
5. For an overview of the persecution of the Church in the first two centuries, see James L. Papandrea, *Reading the Early Church Fathers: From the Didache to Nicaea* (Mahwah, NJ: Paulist Press, 2012), 10–17, 156–60.
6. Ignatius of Antioch, *Letter to the Romans* 3.3. Translation in Holmes, Michael W., *The Apostolic Fathers: Greek Texts and English Translations*, 3rd ed. (Grand Rapids: Baker Academic, 2007), 229.
7. Stark, *Cities of God*, 78, 126–28.
8. Ibid., 187.

9. For more on the Arian controversy, and the resulting ecumenical councils and Nicene Creed, see James L. Papandrea, *Trinity 101: Father, Son, Holy Spirit* (Liguori, MO: Liguori Publications, 2012).

10. Lactantius, *On the Manner in Which the Persecutors Died*, 48.

11. Eusebius of Caesarea, *Life of Constantine* 2.56–60.

12. Constantine was not consistent in applying this policy, however, since he did bring imperial pressure to bear against certain heretical/schismatic groups within the Church. Nevertheless, even during the Arian controversy, his first course of action was diplomatic (writing letters to Bishop Alexander and Arius), and when that didn't work, he convened a council in which he deferred to the authority of the bishops.

13. Eusebius of Caesarea, *Life of Constantine* 2.56.

14. Athanasius of Alexandria, *On the Incarnation* 50–55.

15. By using "ultimate fighting" as an example, we are not criticizing all martial arts. The study of martial arts—for self-defense, exercise, or the building of confidence—is not inherently wrong. Even competitive martial arts, such as one might see in the Olympics, is not wrong. What is morally questionable, however, is the brutality of combat sports in which participants can be seriously and permanently injured in order to provide entertainment for spectators.

16. Many of the early Christian theologians believed that Christians should not attend the "spectacles," which included the gladiator games, circuses, and the theater. Most of the games and theatrical events also included elements of pagan worship and public nudity.

17. A good example of a balanced treatment of the question of how much the United States parallels Rome can be found in Cullen Murphy's book *Are We Rome? The Fall of an Empire and the Fate of America* (Boston: Houghton Mifflin Harcourt, 2007).

18. Papandrea, *The Wedding of the Lamb*, 209–12.

19. There are many places in the world, even today, where persecu-

tion of the Church is violent and is sanctioned by the government. For updates on persecution in the world, see www.opendoorsusa .org, www.persecution.com, and www.redressonline.com. Please note that we do not necessarily endorse or agree with everything on these websites, but they can create an awareness of the ways that violent and oppressive religious persecution continues in the world.

20. The early Christians took Paul's words in Galatians 3:27–28 to heart, rejecting the caste systems of Rome's government and its cults. Though the Church reserves ordination for men, this does not diminish the radical nature of the Church's insistence on the full personhood of every human being. In the present book we are talking about Church membership.

Chapter 2

1. Tertullian, *Apologeticum* 36.4.
2. Thucydides, *Peloponnesian War* 5.89.
3. Norman Cantor, *Antiquity: From the Birth of Sumerian Civilization to the Fall of the Roman Empire* (New York: Harper Perennial), 29.
4. Gerhard Uhlhorn, *Christian Charity in the Ancient Church* (New York: Charles Scribner's Sons, 1883), 3.
5. Saint Cyprian, *Epistle 1*, paragraphs 6–7.
6. Plautus, *Asses*, act 5, scene 2, trans. Paul Nixon, Loeb Classical Library (New York: Putnam, 1916).
7. Seneca, *On Anger* 1:15.
8. Plato, *Republic*, Book 5.
9. Aristotle, *Politics*, Book 8.
10. Naphtali Lewis, *Life in Egypt under Roman Rule* (Oxford, UK: Clarendon, 1983), 54.
11. See F. R. Cowell, *Life in Ancient Rome* (New York: Putnam, 1961), 58.
12. Rodney Stark, *The Rise of Christianity: How the Obscure, Marginal*

Jesus Movement Became the Dominant Religious Force in the Western World in a Few Centuries (San Francisco: HarperCollins, 1997), 97.

13. See the excellent discussion in David Bentley Hart's *Atheist Delusions: The Christian Revolution and Its Fashionable Enemies* (New Haven: Yale, 2009), 166–82.

14. Athenagoras, *Plea for the Christians,* 35.

15. Saint Justin Martyr, *First Apology* 27.

16. *Didascalia Apostolorum* 9.

17. See Vincenzo F. Nicolai, Fabricio Bisconti, and Danilo Mazzoleni, *The Christian Catacombs of Rome: History, Decoration, Inscriptions* (Regensburg, Germany: Verlag Schnell and Steiner, 2002), 147–159.

18. Hilary of Poitiers, *Conflicts of Conscience and Law in the Fourth-Century Church,* trans. Lionel R. Wickham (Liverpool: Liverpool University Press), 51, 101.

Chapter 3

1. Apollodorus, *Library* 1.1–2.1.

2. Quintillian, *Institutio Oratoria* 1.3.16–17.

3. Paul Veyne, *A History of Private Life: From Pagan Rome to Byzantium,* trans. Arthur Goldhammer (Cambridge, MA: Harvard University Press, 1987), 34.

4. Tertullian, *De Spectaculis* 17.5.

5. Tacitus, *Annals* 3.25.

6. Pliny the Younger, *Letters* 4.15.

7. See the excellent discussion of Augustus's failed reform in Patrick Riley, *Civilizing Sex: On Chastity and the Common Good* (Edinburgh: T&T Clark, 2000), 163–74.

8. Clement of Alexandria, *The Instructor* 3.4.

9. *Epistle to Diognetus* 5.

10. Quoted in Richard Walzer, *Galen on Jews and Christians* (London: Oxford University Press, 1949), 65.

11. Celsus, *On True Doctrine.*
12. Saint John Chrysostom, *On Colossians* 12.5.
13. Ibid.
14. Tertullian, *To His Wife,* 2.8.

Chapter 4

1. There is no standard edition of the re-assembled fragments of Celsus's *On True Doctrine.* These quotations are adapted from several translations.
2. Ibid.
3. Ibid.
4. Ibid.
5. Aristotle, *Politics* 1.5.
6. José H. Gomez, "All You Who Labor: Towards a Spirituality of Work for the 21st Century," *Notre Dame Journal of Law, Ethics and Public Policy* 20, no. 2 (2006): 791–814.
7. *Didache* 12.3–4.
8. See the discussion of idleness as a Greco-Roman virtue in Paul Veyne, *A History of Private Life,* 121–37.
9. *Didascalia Apostolorum* 17.
10. *Apostolic Constitutions* 2.8.
11. *Justinian Code* 3.12.3.
12. Saint Basil the Great, *Letters* 207.2.
13. Saint Gregory of Nazianzus, *Orations* 43.63.
14. Saint Basil the Great, *Letters* 262.1.
15. Saint Basil the Great, *Homilies* 338.2.

Chapter 5

1. Colin Brown, ed. *The New International Dictionary of the New Testament,* vol. 1 (Grand Rapids, MI: Zondervan, 1975), 291–307,

s.v. *ekklesia*. Before the time of Jesus, an *ekklesia* (church) was a military or political gathering, but usually with religious elements, such as prayers and sacrifices to the gods, or in the case of Israel, to God.

2. Many biblical scholars would argue that Jesus did not actually say this, because they assume that the word *church* (in Greek, *ekklesia*) is a word he would not have used. The argument goes that since Jesus would not have used the word *church,* then this saying must have been added later by the early Christians who did use the word. This is an example of an argument that begins with its conclusion. Those who want to assume that Jesus didn't say this use the unusual word as "evidence" of that. But can we really assume with such certainty that Jesus would not have used an unusual word? Can we really claim to know what Jesus *wouldn't* have said based on our limited knowledge of what he did say? And didn't Jesus often surprise people by subverting their expectations? We submit that this is another example of that common practice of Jesus—to find new and surprising ways to say things because of the new and surprising things he was doing. Having said that, we also have to remember that Jesus was probably not speaking Greek to his disciples, so he probably did not actually use the Greek word *ekklesia*. So it is entirely possible that the author of the Gospel made the decision to use the word *ekklesia* to translate whatever Aramaic word Jesus actually used. In any case, there is no reason to believe that Jesus did not make this statement about founding the new community that we call the Church, and there is no reason to doubt that Jesus was conscious of the revolutionary nature of what he was doing.

3. We often talk about Pentecost (Acts of the Apostles, chapter 2) as the birth of the Church, but we would like to suggest that Pentecost was really more like the confirmation of the Church. Its baptism was the death and resurrection of Jesus Christ, and Its birth was the night Jesus gathered his disciples around a table and said, "Do this in remembrance of me." Long before

the Church had anything to do with an institution, or even a building, the Church was defined as those who gathered around the table and received Christ in the Eucharist (in union with the apostles and their successors).

4. Interestingly, one Egyptian pharaoh tried to shift Egypt toward a version of monotheism (sun worship), possibly influenced by the Hebrew slaves in Egypt. But the idea didn't take hold, and after his death, Egypt reverted to polytheism.

5. See James L. Papandrea, "Jesus Saw It Coming—The Gospels and Revelation," in *The Wedding of the Lamb: A Historical Approach to the Book of Revelation* (Eugene, OR: Pickwick Publications, 2011).

6. Justin Martyr, *On the Resurrection,* excerpts from chapters 2, 4, 8, and 9.

7. To be clear, polytheism must not be confused with the ancient Christian practice of praying to the saints and asking for their intercession. In the Christian tradition, only God is divine, and therefore, only God is to be worshipped. Furthermore, it is precisely because God is divine, and therefore omnipresent and omnipotent, that there is no room for other gods. God does not share authority with any other heavenly being. The saints are human beings, and for that reason they are not worshipped. The tradition of praying to the saints is a devotional practice in which the saints are invited to join in the prayers of the people—all prayers being directed ultimately to God. The living pray with the saints, and the saints pray for the living, but the saints are never worshipped, nor is divine power ever attributed to them.

8. See James L. Papandrea, "The Doctrine of the Trinity," in *Trinity 101: Father, Son, Holy Spirit* (Liguori, MO: Liguori Publications, 2012), 64–93.

9. See Papandrea, "The Trinity in Scripture," in *Trinity 101,* 9–63.

10. By "mainstream" Church, we mean the majority of the Church, represented by those apologists, bishops, and theologians who

clarified doctrine, often in response to challenges from fringe groups that denied or diminished one of the two natures of Jesus Christ.

11. For a more detailed treatment of early apostolic succession, along with examples of opposition to it, see James L. Papandrea, *Reading the Early Church Fathers: From the Didache to Nicaea* (Mahwah, NJ: Paulist Press, 2012), 48–54, 58–82, 139–54.

12. For a more detailed definition of the concept of consubstantiality, see Papandrea, *Trinity 101*, 106–8.

13. See Papandrea, "The Nicene Creed," in *Trinity 101*, 94–123.

14. Tertullian, *Apology* 13.

15. It could be argued that some forms of Buddhism include a philosophy of care for others, and it is not our intention to dismiss that; however, it was only the Christian version of love of neighbor that would convert the world.

16. See James L. Papandrea, "Introduction: The Five Homes and the Image of God," in *Spiritual Blueprint: How We Live, Work, Love, Play, and Pray* (Liguori, MO: Liguori Publications, 2010), vii–xi.

17. Tertullian, *Apology* 18.

18. Papandrea, *Reading the Early Church Fathers,* 156–75.

19. Ibid., 176–83, 207–10.

20. The equality of all believers was affirmed in terms of each person's worth—that every person was deserving of protection, respect, and equal access to resources. Here we are talking about the membership of the Church, not the leadership of the Church, as it was assumed that only men could be ordained to the clergy offices of bishop, priest, and deacon. Although it was not the case that all members could be clergy, this does not diminish the important fact that the Church rejected distinctions of race and class. The offices of deaconess, consecrated virgin, and widow existed as official ministries of women, in addition to the general expectation that all laypeople were to participate in the ministry of the Church.

21. The early Christians believed that there was no way to encounter

Christ apart from the sacraments. Some said that God could theoretically save anyone he wants, but that did not diminish the fact that salvation was normatively found in the sacraments: this is how the believer connects with Christ, identifies with Christ, and remains in Christ. This is why they believed that there was no salvation outside the Church.

22. On rebaptism, see Papandrea, *Trinity 101*, 88–90.

Chapter 6

1. There was, of course, a diverse array of philosophical schools in the ancient world, each with its own code of ethics. The followers of some ancient philosophies, such as the Pythagoreans and Cynics, sought to renounce wealth, but this was not a matter of adopting simple living for the benefit of others. It was a rejection of society and social relationships. Some others, such as the Sophists, taught that morality is relative, based on what is best for the individual—ultimately a self-serving utilitarianism. A philosophical school known as the Skeptics took that idea to its logical conclusion and taught that right and wrong are not universal, but in fact are creations of particular cultures, so that what is wrong for one culture may be right for another. This form of relativism exists to this day, but its fatal flaw was demonstrated in the twentieth century when it became clear that cultural relativism leaves no basis on which to critique genocide.

2. For a slightly more detailed treatment of the controversy, see James L. Papandrea, *Reading the Early Church Fathers: From the Didache to Nicaea* (Mahwah, NJ: Paulist Press, 2012), 200–207. Pelagius's teachings were condemned as heresy. The Church's conclusions were finally clarified at the Council of Orange, in the year 529.

3. Mike Aquilina, *Yours Is the Church: How Catholicism Shapes Our World* (Cincinnati: Servant Books, 2012), 32. See also Helen

Rhee, *Loving the Poor, Saving the Rich: Wealth, Poverty, and Early Christian Formation* (Grand Rapids, MI: Baker, 2012), 18.

4. Rhee, *Loving the Poor, Saving the Rich,* 18–19. See also David Batson, *The Treasure Chest of the Early Christians: Faith, Care and Community from the Apostolic Age to Constantine the Great* (Grand Rapids, MI: Eerdmans, 2001), 21.

5. Batson, *The Treasure Chest of the Early Christians,* 35.

6. Ibid., 27. Of course, the Jews also had a tradition of almsgiving, as well as responsibility for caring for the widow, orphan, and sojourner, but the Christian version of charity converted the world.

7. See Hermas, *The Shepherd* 17.5–6, 27.4–7, 50–51.

8. The late first-century catechesis document known as *The Didache* states, "Do not claim that anything is your own." *Didache* 4.8.

9. Rhee, *Loving the Poor, Saving the Rich,* 58–64, 101–2. Note that almsgiving is a penance—it is not something that earns salvation or creates a relationship with God. It is something that helps those who are already in a relationship with God through Christ "remain in" him (John 15:1–10).

10. Batson, *The Treasure Chest of the Early Christians,* 57.

11. Hermas, *The Shepherd* 27.4–7. See also *Didache* 4.6. Notice the emphasis on the family; this is not merely an individual enterprise; the Christian life is lived in community, in families, and in the Church. Even when it comes to working out our salvation, we are not alone; we do that in community. This is related to the concept of vicarious faith. The faith of one's family can support the individual where his or her faith is lacking, as we see with infant baptism.

12. *2 Clement* 16.4.

13. Cyprian of Carthage, *On the Lapsed* 35.

14. Justin Martyr, *The First Apology* 67. See also Aquilina, *Yours Is the Church,* 33–34; and Batson, *The Treasure Chest of the Early Christians,* 115–16. Whenever early preachers thought that the

wealthy Christians were being stingy, sermons exhorted them to share.

15. See James L. Papandrea, *Rome: A Pilgrim's Guide to the Eternal City* (Eugene, OR: Cascade Books, 2012), 117–26.

16. The letter is preserved in Eusebius of Caesarea, *Ecclesiastical History* 6.43.

17. See Aquilina, *Yours Is the Church*, 38–40. The monasteries of Europe became hostels, hospitals, and hospice wards, as well as schools.

18. Ibid., 35. The care that Christians provided to non-Christians often resulted in the conversion of many people who witnessed the bravery and compassion of the Christians.

19. Rhee, *Loving the Poor, Saving the Rich*, 180.

20. Admittedly, this notion infected some parts of the Church, especially in the medieval period.

21. See Lactantius, *Epitome of Divine Institutes* 39. Suicide was always considered a sin, since it is a form of murder. But the Church formally condemned suicide at a council in the city of Arles in the year 452.

22. Rhee, *Loving the Poor, Saving the Rich*, 78–79. Note that since almsgiving was commanded, some surplus wealth was necessary or there would be nothing to give to the poor.

23. The heretics in question are the Gnostics. They reasoned that since the material world was beneath consideration, so were the material needs of other people. See Rhee, *Loving the Poor, Saving the Rich*, 205.

24. Ibid., 6–7, 18–19, 26–27.

Chapter 7

1. *Martyrdom of Polycarp* 17–18.

2. *The Odyssey of Homer*, trans. William Cowper (London: J. M. Dent & Sons, 1791), book 11, vv. 593–97.

3. Julian, *Epistle* 67 (To the People of Antioch).
4. Saint Ambrose of Milan, *Letters* 22.
5. Saint Augustine, *Confessions* 9.11.
6. Saint Augustine, *On the Care of the Dead* 4.
7. Ibid., 5–6.

Chapter 8

1. The expression "American experiment" is usually credited to Alexis de Tocqueville, based on his 1835 book *Democracy in America*. The phrase was inspired by a line in George Washington's 1789 inaugural address. Washington said that this new country was going to be a nation that acknowledged the authority of a higher power and held itself accountable to God.

2. Human nature being what it is, many Christian rulers fell back into this kind of thinking in later centuries. As we will see, the Constantinian experiment was short-lived, but it was not for that reason any less important.

3. See the discussion on the number 666 and the "mark of the beast," in James L. Papandrea, *The Wedding of the Lamb: A Historical Approach to the Book of Revelation* (Eugene, OR: Pickwick Publications, 2011), 34–36, 133–36, 156–59.

4. For a discussion of the development of the hierarchy in the early Church, see James L. Papandrea, *Reading the Early Church Fathers: From the Didache to Nicaea* (Mahwah, NJ: Paulist Press, 2012), 48–54. Also see the discussion on *apostolic succession*, pp. 21–22.

5. There is some evidence that Clement of Rome (bishop from 88 to 97) was a slave in the early years of his episcopacy. It is true that women could not be ordained to the three clergy offices of bishop, priest, and deacon. But this was for other reasons, beyond the scope of the present book, and it was still the case that

women had religious vocations open to them, including the offices of widow, deaconess, and consecrated virgin.

6. Tertullian, *On Idolatry* 19; *On the Resurrection of the Flesh* 16.
See also Origen, *Against Celsus* 7.26; and the *Apostolic Tradition* 16.17. Often these condemnations of capital punishment are
voiced in the context of an argument that Christians should not
be soldiers—an argument that would all but go away after the
rise of Constantine. See also Athenagoras, *A Plea for the Christians* 35, which could be interpreted as a condemnation of capital punishment.

7. Athenagoras, *A Plea for the Christians* 35.

8. Novatian, *On the Spectacles* 4.

9. Tertullian, *Apology* 24.

10. There are at least three different churches dedicated to St. Lawrence (San Lorenzo) in Rome. See James L. Papandrea, *Rome: A
Pilgrim's Guide to the Eternal City* (Eugene, OR: Cascade Books,
2012), 102–7.

11. See Eusebius of Caesarea, *Life of Constantine* 1.16–17, where Eusebius says that Constantius (Constantine's father) was indeed a
Christian, and 2.49, where the testimony of Constantius's faith
comes from Constantine himself.

12. The story is preserved in Eusebius of Caesarea, *Life of Constantine* 1.28–31, as well as in Lactantius, *Of the Manner in Which
the Persecutors Died* 44. In Eusebius, Constantine saw a vision of
a cross in the sky, but in Lactantius, Constantine had a dream
in which he saw the Chi-Rho monogram. This looks like a
capital X superimposed over a capital P, but it is really the two
Greek letters Chi (X) and Rho (P), the first two letters of *Chris-
tos*, the Greek word for "Christ." It is more likely that the original story was that Constantine saw the Chi-Rho, since the cross
was not yet being widely used as a symbol of the Church.

13. The victory is remembered with the commemoration of Milvian
Bridge Day, on October 28.

14. This is the inscription on the inside of the central archway of the Arch of Constantine, near the Colosseum in Rome.

15. Tertullian, *Apology* 24.

16. Josephus, *Antiquities of the Jews* 18.3.4.

17. Ibid., 18.3.1. Cf. Luke 13:1–2.

18. Ibid., 18.3.5.

19. Lactantius, *Of the Manner in Which the Persecutors Died* 48.

20. Eusebius of Caesarea, *Life of Constantine* 2.48–60.

21. Ibid., 2.56.

22. See Papandrea, *The Wedding of the Lamb,* 161–67, 234–35.

23. Both the cult of Mithras and various gnostic groups included imitations of Christian eucharistic rites in their litanies. Justin Martyr, *First Apology* 66. See also Rodney Stark, *Cities of God: The Real Story of How Christianity Became an Urban Movement and Conquered Rome* (New York: HarperOne, 2006), 187.

24. For example, it is often said that December 25 was a pagan holiday before it was a Christian holiday. The truth is that the date of December 25 for the birth of Christ comes from a calculation of nine months after the Feast of the Annunciation, March 25. The date was established as the birthday of Jesus (in the West) at least from the early third century, but probably much earlier. The date did not become attached to Sol Invictus (the sun god) until the reign of the emperor Aurelian, in the late third century. Clearly, Aurelian's intention was to take the date away from the Christians and establish a pagan celebration on that day.

25. It is important to note that another myth about Constantine— that he pressured the bishops at Nicaea to accept the doctrine of the Trinity (or worse, that he had a hand in creating the doctrine)—is also untrue. Constantine did convene the council, and he did have an agenda there which was a quick settlement of the Arian controversy and the preservation of the unity of the Church. But in his letter to Arius and his bishop, Alexander, Constantine demonstrated that he did not understand

the doctrinal issues at stake and considered the whole thing a minor matter. Going into the council, Constantine did not push for one outcome or another—only that some conclusion must be forthcoming to put an end to the division in the Church. Therefore, we cannot attribute the "victory" of the doctrine of the Trinity at Nicaea to the power of Constantine. We can, however, assume that once the doctrine was established as orthodox and consistent with Scripture and prior tradition, Constantine did have some influence on those bishops who wanted to dissent, and most of them signed the creed under his watchful eye.

26. The creed of Nicaea-Constantinople is the same as our western Nicene Creed, with the exception of the words *and the Son* (the Holy Spirit "proceeds from the Father *and the Son*"), which were added later, and only in the West. See James L. Papandrea, *Trinity 101: Father, Son, Holy Spirit* (Liguori, MO: Liguori Publications, 2012), especially the section on the explanation of the Nicene Creed.

27. See Cullen Murphy's interesting book *Are We Rome? The Fall of an Empire and the Fate of America* (Boston: Houghton Mifflin Harcourt, 2007).

28. Ibid., 16.

29. Admittedly, it could be argued that we as a nation do engage in certain forms of colonization, including economic colonization. Nevertheless, the point remains that to the extent that we do not colonize, we reduce the risk of spreading ourselves too thin. And if it can be argued that involvement in certain conflicts on foreign soil constitutes a form of colonialism, then the experience of the Roman Empire should provide a cautionary tale.

30. Murphy, *Are We Rome?* 16.

31. M. E. Bradford, *A Worthy Company: Brief Lives of the Framers of the United States Constitution* (Marlborough, NH: Plymouth Rock Foundation, 1982), ix.

32. Ibid., ix–x.

33. In the time before the Establishment Clause, several colonies did not allow Catholics freedom of worship.
34. See Papandrea, *Wedding of the Lamb*, 200–206.
35. Murphy, *Are We Rome?* 178.

Chapter 9

1. Thomas F. Farr, "Our Failed Religious Freedom Policy," *First Things* (November 2013), pp. 35–40. As mentioned above, there have been some recent victories for religious freedom, including a few encouraging Supreme Court decisions, but the opponents of religious freedom are currently devising ways to circumvent those Supreme Court decisions, and they are continually proposing laws that would restrict religious freedom. Sadly, even self-proclaimed Christians in Congress support these laws under the false conviction that they are necessary for "separation of church and state." At this point, the Church cannot afford to be anything less than vigilant.
2. Michael J. Gorman, *Abortion and the Early Church: Christian, Jewish and Pagan Attitudes in the Greco-Roman World* (Eugene, OR: Wipf & Stock, 1998), 98. Worldwide, the annual number of abortions is over forty million, which—as some have noted—qualifies abortion as a kind of holocaust. See John Powell, *Abortion: The Silent Holocaust* (Allen, TX: Argus, 1981).
3. Abortion for gender selection is difficult to quantify. Although we might normally associate the practice with countries such as China and India, evidence suggests that this practice occurs in the United States, perhaps in large part among immigrants from those cultures. See Jason Abrevaya, "Are There Missing Girls in the United States? Evidence from Birth Data," *American Economic Journal: Applied Economics* 1, no. 2 (April 2009): 1–34.
4. What may have begun in many people's awareness as the at-

tempt to remove religious symbols and lists of the Ten Commandments from government buildings is now becoming more acute in the context of health care and its intersection with business. See Kyle Duncan, "How Fares Religious Freedom," *First Things* (October 2013), 20–22.

5. See Rémi Brague, "The Impossibility of Secular Society," *First Things* (October 2013), 27–31.

6. In a practical sense, discussions about how to change worship and liturgy to attract more people are missing the point. Congregations that bend over backward to be relevant are in fact capitulating to the very cultural trends that are here today and gone tomorrow. What people really need is something more timeless that will stand out amidst the ever-fluctuating fads of "relevance."

7. Athanasius, *Life of Anthony* 78.

8. See James L. Papandrea, *The Wedding of the Lamb: A Historical Approach to the Book of Revelation* (Eugene, OR: Pickwick Publications, 2011), 165–66.

Chapter 10

1. See James L. Papandrea, *Spiritual Blueprint: How We Live, Work, Love, Play, and Pray* (Liguori, MO: Liguori Publications, 2010), 78–80.

2. Michael J. Gorman, *Abortion and the Early Church: Christian, Jewish and Pagan Attitudes in the Greco-Roman World* (Eugene, OR: Wipf & Stock, 1998), 22–23, 32, 77, 82, 84–85, 94.

3. For suggestions about how to integrate creativity into life, and find more fulfillment through self-expression, see Papandrea, *Spiritual Blueprint*.

4. Rémi Brague, "The Impossibility of a Secular Society," *First Things* (October 2013), 27–31.

5. See Thomas F. Farr, "Our Failed Religious Freedom Policy," *First Things* (November 2013), 35–40.
6. For more information on persecution of Christians worldwide, see the websites www.persecution.com, and www.opendoorsusa .org.

An excerpt from

THE ANCIENT PATH

by Michael Talbot with Mike Aquilina

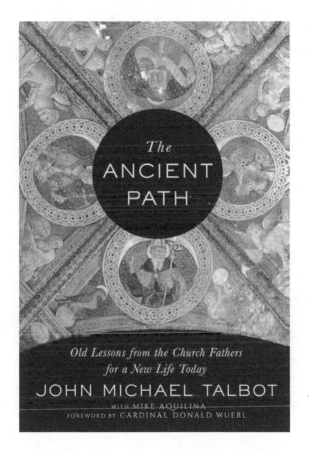

The
ANCIENT
PATH

Old Lessons from the Church Fathers
for a New Life Today

JOHN MICHAEL TALBOT

WITH MIKE AQUILINA
FOREWORD BY CARDINAL DONALD WUERL

978-0-8041-3995-3 • $22.00 / CAN $26.00

Also available as an ebook

IMAGE

Chapter 1

YOU CAN BECOME ALL FIRE

T HE MONASTERY WHERE I LIVE, LITTLE PORTION
Hermitage, nestles in a wooded valley off a rural route
in the Ozark Mountains of northern Arkansas. Our
community lives in solitude, far from the nearest streetlights or
porch lights. At night the sky is filled with stars, and you can
count them if you have the time. Our woods, though, are so
dark that you can't see much beyond two feet in front of you.

In such a place, with such deep, dark nights, you come to
appreciate the force of the Gospel's simple observation "It was
night" (see John 13:30; also John 3:2). Night is the time when
the wild beasts enjoy their brief advantage over human intel-
ligence. They can see us; we can't see them. They can move
easily through the terrain. Our every footfall is a guess—and a
potential pratfall.

April 29, 2008, was just such a night. It was after eleven,
and I was wrapping up my tasks for the day, a bit later than
usual. My wife, Viola, was already asleep in bed. Our hermit-

age, like all the homes at the monastery, is a "green" building. Partially underground, it retains heat well in the winter and keeps pleasantly cool in the summer. Its great source of light by day is a skylight in the roof.

It was something about the skylight that startled me when I looked up from my desk. It should have been black with the night, but it was radiant—with a golden-orange glow.

Well, that's really strange, I thought.

My tired mind reached for implausible explanations as I headed for the door. *Maybe there's a problem with the well, and the utility crew is working late.*

Just three steps beyond my door I knew that the glow was nothing so benign. I felt intense heat. And I looked up to see the whole back end of the common building of our community— just a hundred yards from my hermitage—engulfed in flames.

The golden glow I had seen in the skylight? It was the immolation of our chapel, our library, our business offices, and the refectory where we share our simple meals.

My community is the Brothers and Sisters of Charity, and we have been living together since 1979, first on the grounds of Alverna Retreat Center in Indianapolis, and then, since 1982, on our grounds in Arkansas. We built the structures with our own hands from native stone and good wood. We built the *community* with similarly seasoned materials—the heritage of early Christianity, the traditions of Christian communal life. So we built our monastery as much with books as with blocks.

We weren't born in the valley where we now live. We converged there, came intentionally as disciples. The road we took was not just that rural route in the Ozarks, but a far more ancient path, the way of the Fathers.

We are a community that integrates families, singles who are free to marry, and traditional consecrated celibates. Our configuration is rare, if not unique, in modern times. But we fashioned it on models we found in the fourth century, when Christians in many lands undertook great experiments in living common life. Even as we built our buildings, we pored over the long-ago eyewitness accounts of the lives of Anthony of the Desert, Pachomius, John Cassian, Basil the Great, and the Fathers of the Egyptian desert. They and their companions fled the cities of the Greco-Roman world in order to make communities for intentional contemplative living. They succeeded so well—and built so sturdily—that many of their monasteries are still standing today, in spite of persecutions, and in spite of many centuries of natural disasters (what the insurance companies call "acts of God").

You can also see "monuments" of those ancient builders in the later experiments of Bernard of Clairvaux, Francis of Assisi, Dominic de Guzmán, and Ignatius of Loyola. The saints depend upon the saints; the Fathers took up what the apostles had handed on; the apostles learned the ways of common life from Jesus.

From the first generation it has been so. "And they devoted themselves to the apostles' teaching and fellowship, to the breaking of bread and the prayers. . . . And all who believed were together and had all things in common and they sold their possessions and goods and distributed them to all, as any had need" (Acts 2:42, 44-45).

If you spotted the ancient monasteries from a helicopter

high above, you would be looking down on an ancient Christian commentary on the Scriptures. If you took a few turns and flew over Little Portion Hermitage, you could look down at our own particular reflection on the Gospel. We built the Gospel, as we saw it, into the layout of our roads and roofs.

Our monastery, as I said, consists of a large common building, surrounded by small habitations—hermitages—where individuals and families pass their days in quiet work and prayer and in solitude with God.

———

Maybe you can imagine, then, what passed through my mind in the instant when I recognized what was happening to our common building at the monastery. I stepped out of my hermitage to see the work of so many years, the work of our hearts and minds and hands, going up in flames.

At first I thought I would rush in and save what I could from the chapel. But I saw right away that the flames rose highest in the back end. The chapel—with its altar, tabernacle, and the choir stalls where we pray—was already gone. The vestments and vessels used in the sacred liturgy were gone. The icons were gone. So was my office, with all the community's records from thirty years of family life, and the awards and mementos of forty years of making music, and every photograph I had of my childhood, my late parents, my past.

I turned back to wake Viola. We ran, stumbling, in the darkness to every hermitage, banging on the doors and shouting, "Fire! Fire!" We called 911, but knew it would be a while before any emergency vehicles could make their way to our secluded valley.

I hurried back in the direction of the big building and impulsively rushed inside. It was thick with black smoke. I couldn't see anything and soon felt I was going to pass out. I went back outside for air, then back in, but I was unable to retrieve anything. I did this a few times before giving up entirely.

By now the whole community was there and feeling frantic. I realized our efforts were futile. So I said: "Let it burn. Let it burn. It's not worth anybody getting hurt. Let it burn."

We all walked down to the grove to wait for the fire department. We just kind of stood there, listening to the fire roar, pop, and boom, and we tried to let go of it all.

There came one particularly loud boom, and we began to see dozens—and then hundreds—of what looked like little butterflies hovering around us. They were beautiful embers of light. And we realized that they were paper.

"There goes the library," someone said. "There it goes."

And that's when I felt the loss—thousands of volumes, the repository of so much knowledge and tradition, stored lovingly in bank upon bank of stocked bookshelves.

The "butterflies" flitting around us were pages of Cyprian, Origen, Athanasius, Augustine—my spiritual and intellectual companions as I founded the community. The books, with all my marginal notes, were gone.

—

A fire is a catastrophic loss, and you feel it immediately. Emergency crews worked through the night and overcame the blaze, but it was not long before we began to realize the extent of our losses. Kind neighbors brought us food—but we had no utensils to eat with!

To this day I still begin to walk to the library to retrieve a particular book, only to remember halfway that it isn't there.

Yet I'm also coming to realize that I still have it all. Perhaps my bond with the ancient Fathers is closer than ever.

Early on, when I realized I no longer had my volumes of the Fathers close at hand, it occurred to me that the Fathers themselves owned very few books. Even for their spiritual descendants in the Middle Ages, books were a rare luxury. There were no printing presses—and certainly no electronic media: no audiobooks, podcasts, software, or websites. Saint Thomas Aquinas once said longingly that he would give all of Paris for just a single volume of Saint John Chrysostom's sermons.

I know that feeling! But I also know that I have what I need of the Fathers. After spending so many years steeped in their lives, I find that their words and ideas arise often in my mind and my prayer. If I have the impulse to reach for their writings, it's because I want to complete a thought already begun. I want to remember where the Fathers went from there.

One of the great lessons I'm still learning from the Fathers is detachment from things, even the best of things—even the beautiful words of the Fathers.

After losing all those thousands of volumes, I'm finding that the witness of the Fathers remains with me, and in many ways it is stronger now than ever. That's the witness I want to share in this book. This book is my "handing on"—that's the literal meaning of the Latin word at the root of *tradition*. We take what our Fathers have given us and pass it along to the next generation.

This book is my retrieval of the companionship of these great men, who have exercised a true fatherhood—a spiritual fatherhood—in my life. I have learned to walk the ancient path because I followed after them, like a little son, watching what they did and trying to learn from them and imitate them.

I think of Saint John Cassian, the great monastic father of the fifth century, and how he spent his youth among the "athletes of prayer" in the Egyptian desert. Later he traveled to France, where he founded monasteries and set down his memories of the great men and women he had met and the lessons they had taught him.

It's my turn now, and I hope you, too, will take your turn. First, before we do our "handing on," we need to receive what the great tradition has carefully kept for us. This book is my act of retrieval and recovery, taking up again what I once received, and sharing the joy of that rediscovery with you, dear friend, as we walk the ancient path together.

There is an enigmatic story preserved in the sayings of the Desert Fathers, from fourth-century Egypt.

> Abba Lot went to see Abba Joseph and said to him: "Abba, as far as I can I say my little office, I fast a little, I pray and meditate, I live in peace as far as I can, I purify my thoughts. What else can I do?" Then the old man stood up and stretched his hands towards heaven. His fingers became like ten lamps of fire and he said to him, "If you will, you can become all flame."[1]

I had consumed all those many books long before the fire consumed them. The last time I saw them, they had indeed "become all flame." Now I need to become what I found in them. I need to become all fire, with a blaze that can consume the world (see Luke 12:49).